WIN AT
CHECKERS

WIN AT
CHECKERS

By MILLARD HOPPER

———

DOVER PUBLICATIONS, INC.

NEW YORK

Published in Canada by General Publishing Company, Ltd., 30 Lesmill Road, Don Mills, Toronto, Ontario.
Published in the United Kingdom by Constable and Company, Ltd.

This Dover edition, first published in 1956, is a revised version of the work originally published in 1941 by A. S. Barnes under the title *Checkers, All the Answers on the Art of Successful Checker Playing.*

International Standard Book Number: 0-486-20363-8

Library of Congress Catalog Card Number: 57-13536

Manufactured in the United States of America
Dover Publications, Inc.
180 Varick Street
New York, N. Y. 10014

DEDICATED TO MY WIFE

ELENORE FOX,

WHOSE CONSTANT ENCOURAGEMENT

HAS BEEN A GREAT ASSISTANCE

TO ME IN MY TASKS

Is it necessary to have a special talent to become a checker expert?

This is one of the questions asked me almost every day. The answer is *No*. Checker ability demands no special talent or faculties outside of average intelligence.

If anyone is desirous of mastering the game and willing to devote a little time to learning its principles, he will have little difficulty in becoming an expert player. In addition, he will find himself amply rewarded for Checkers carries a fascination unequaled by any other game.

Someone once said "The game of Checkers will never die," certainly it has stood the test of time; first of all because it's fun and entertainment, but also because it teaches foresight, caution, and the ability to think quickly and clearly.

It is recognized by Churchmen, Educators and Psychologists as a sound character builder and lifetime hobby. Once learned, its devotees may never fear the dullness of idle moments, and its infinite variety of play holds an ever-present enchantment.

Thousands of hospitals and sanitariums are using checkers for its therapeutic effect and the game is recommended by leading physicians for the convalescent and depressed.

The eminent New York intestinal specialist Dr. Joseph Franklin Montague in his recent interesting book entitled *Broadway Stomach,* recommends checkers as a hobby for the overcoming of frustration and other emotional disturbances. No matter how healthy you are, you will find restful relaxation in a pleasant game—and as long as you are going to play, why not learn to play well?

Today, in millions of homes throughout the country Checkers is the leading pastime. At Clubs, Parks and Playgrounds, youth and age alike sit down to indulge in a friendly game.

Even the streamlined Hollywood movie stars have become Checker-minded and find the game an ideal pastime between the sets.

In Post Offices, Firehouses, and Police Stations, Checkers has always been the standard spare time sport.

Unlike many other games, Checkers knows no season, and no country. It is played in one form or other in almost every country on the globe. Unfortunately, however, while millions play the game, most checker fans have one thing in common—they don't know how to play the game well. Most of them play a "hit-and-miss" haphazard game trusting to luck and their opponent's oversights to bring victory.

Actually, checkers is a highly scientific game and every move from start to finish should be made with a purpose in mind. Just watch an expert knock the daylight out of a beginner, and you will realize he has got something that has no demand for luck or oversights. Skill is the fundamental basis of the game and this skill can only be attained by learning these certain principles and strategies.

The latest World War has given great impetus to the game. In training camps, hospitals, and underground bomb shelters, checkers supplies a blessed relief from the rigors of modern warfare. In many ways the game exemplifies the tactics of battle, and some of the leading military generals of the past developed their ingenuity through the strategies of the game. Napoleon, the Duke of Wellington, Frederick the Great were all great checker players, and General U. S. Grant whose ability to mop up the boys at West Point is well recorded, ascribed much of his military success to the mental sharpening derived from the game.

What a better world to live in, if all the battles could have been fought out over the checkered board with mobilized wooden pieces, rather than on shell-torn fields and cities at the sacrifice of human lives.

CONTENTS

■■■

WIN AT
CHECKERS

....

CHAPTER ONE

A REVIEW OF THE
GENERAL PRINCIPLES OF THE GAME

Just to give you an idea of how one of my students becomes transformed from a "hit-and-miss" checker player into a competent devotee of the game, consider the following conversation as though you were listening in on a discussion between the student and myself.

Mr. Hopper, is there any rule as to who moves first in the game?

Yes, there is a definite rule that the Black checkers always have the first move in a game. On the following game, the players change colors so that the first move alternates with each game.

I know in a general way that checkers is a game played on squares by opposing groups of twelve checkers, but let's assume that I know nothing other than that. I want you to tell me precisely what the object of the game is.

The object of checkers is to capture or block all of your opponent's men, in which case you win the game.

How may this be accomplished?

This may be accomplished in several ways. First, by breaking through your opponent's ranks, securing the first King and using it to capture and destroy your opponent's single checkers. Secondly, by gaining a superior number of pieces by getting your opponent in a shot or trap, and thirdly, by so maneuvering your men that your opponent's men are either blocked, or his pieces pinned so that he is unable to move.

What is the numbered checkerboard? and what part does it play in becoming a checker expert?

The Numbered Checkerboard might be termed the Reference Chart of Checker science. It is only by this system of numbering the playing squares of the board that the various moves can be pointed out and recorded. The numbers merely indicate the different squares on the playing field and makes it possible to designate the position of the checkers.

By the aid of the Numbered Board, the student, or player can keep a complete record of all the moves of a game, thus enabling him to play the game over later and locate his mistakes.

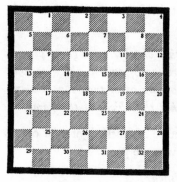

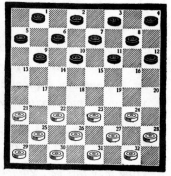

DIAG. 1. The Numbered Checkerboard.

DIAG. 1A. The men set up for play.

The diagrams herewith show the Numbered Checkerboard with the checkers set up for play. The board is numbered from one to thirty-two in consecutive order, and the

Black checkers always occupy the low numbered squares from 1 to 12, at the start of the game. The White pieces as shown occupy squares from 21 to 32.

What is meant by the "double corner," and "single corner" on the board?

The "Double Corner" means the corner of the board where there are two playing squares instead of one. Black's Double Corner is composed of squares 1 and 5. White's Double Corner is squares 32 and 28.

The Single Corner is the corner with the single playing squares and is always at your left as you face the board. White's Single Corner is square 29, and Black's Single Corner is square 4.

Generally speaking, which is the weakest part of your opponent's forces?

Generally speaking, the weakest part of your opponent's forces is on his Double Corner side of the board. This is on the left hand side of the board as you advance. Usually the first King is secured on this side of the board, White getting his King on square 1, and Black securing his King on square 32.

Is it good policy to exchange pieces as rapidly as possible in order to reduce the number of men? This is the popular impression. Is there any truth in it?

To exchange men simply to cut down the number of pieces generally leads to a weak or lost game. An exchange of men should only be made when it accomplishes some definite purpose: either to remove your opponent's men which are blocking your advance, or where it gives you a commanding position that will enable you to run a checker through for a King.

On the other hand, my thought is that if the double corner is the weakest side of the board, why shouldn't I exchange in that direction to decimate or kill off all the checkers on that side of the board; thus leaving an open path to my opponent's King row?

It is a good policy to exchange in that direction, but first your men must be moved into position in the center of the board to prepare for these exchanges.

How can I tell when it is the proper time to make an exchange?

When you are certain the rest of your position is safe from immediate attack, and when you see a definite advantage to be gained.

Is there any zone or squares which possess more strategic importance than others?

Yes, the central squares of the board are known as Key Squares. These squares are the ones numbered 14, 15, 18, and 19.

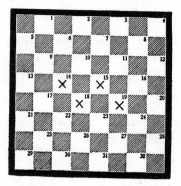

DIAG. 2. The Key Squares.

To occupy these squares gives you a general advantage of position. However, in occupying these squares you must have supporting checkers, and these must be in a position to be brought forward without acting as a detriment to your back-field defense.

When I am once in possession of this strategic area, what use can I make of it to break into my opponent's king row?

Once in possession of these squares you have an opportunity to impede your opponent's advancing men, likewise these central squares can be used as a spearhead to attack and advance your own men.

In other words—when I am once in possession of these squares, or bases, is it then to my advantage to trade "blow for blow"?

Yes, it is to your advantage to trade blow for blow; however, these blows should be so timed that they will land at a time when they will cause the most damage.

Is there any general rule you can give me for the estimation of my opponent's position and weaknesses?

By looking for holes or weak spots in your opponent's ranks you can tell just when and where to attack. A broken up position with straggling men should be attacked with full force. The following diagrams show two instances where this rule applies.

DIAG. 3. White to move.

In Diagram 3, Black's ranks are weakest on your right side of the board, the vacant squares on 3, 8, and 11 forming a big hole or gap. White's best play is to smash at this weak point, and he plays 24-19; an exchange that further disrupts Black's game.

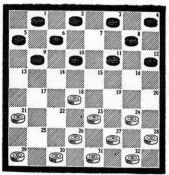

DIAG. 4. White to move.

In Diagram 4, Black's weak point is the hole on square 7, and White occupying the center of the board can attack that point by moving 18 to 15. Make the exchange of men, and note how Black's forces are divided. It is difficult to rebuild a new and sound defense after having your ranks broken in this manner. Whenever you can split your opponent's forces with an exchange in this manner it is a technical advantage.

How can I avoid these holes and weak spots in my own ranks?

By consolidating your pieces as you move forward. Each man should be moved towards the center of the board in a wedge-shaped formation. As a checker is moved forward it should be backed up by another checker from your secondary line of men. This will keep your checkers in a compact mass and avoid holes or weak spots in your defense.

The following diagram shows a solid wedge-shaped advance by the Black checkers. Black has moved from 11 to 15, then from 8 to 11, and finally from 4 to 8. Each checker has backed up the one ahead and Black has made a complete advance down the center of the board keeping his men in a solid, compact formation.

DIAG. 5. The "Single Corner" advance.

With the White checkers, the same Single Corner advance can be obtained by moving 22-18, 25-22, and 29-25.

These Single Corner advances are the strongest opening attacks in checkers.

Suppose my opponent moves his men forward in this solid single corner attack, what is the best defense against it?

The strongest defense against it is an exchange of men, which breaks up the spearhead of his advance and slows up his attack—for instance, after Black led off with 11-15, White could reply 22-18, immediately breaking up his control of the center of the board. After the exchanges, when Black reforms his men you do likewise, backing up your forward men and watching carefully to see which side of his board is least protected. (This Opening is gone into fully in a later chapter.)

Say, this is fascinating! By the way, how old is the game of checkers?

Older than you would suppose; in fact, checkers is the oldest game in the world and dates back over 4000 years. According to inscriptions in the temples of Thebes, the Egyptian kings took time out from building the Pyramids to mop up their courtiers at Checkers.

In Homer's Odyssey, reference is made to games being played in the palace of Ulysses in Ithaca; also Plato makes frequent mention of the games in his writings.

Down through the years the game has held its perennial appeal, being played by great and humble folk alike. The earliest book on the game was published by Antonio Torquemada, a Spanish author at Valencia, Spain, in the year 1547.

Were there many famous people of the past who were fond of checkers?

Yes, George Washington, Benjamin Franklin, and Abraham Lincoln were noted for their love of checkers. Edgar Allan Poe and the famous lexicographer Samuel Johnson considered the game superior to all educational pastimes.

Who were some of the later day devotees of the game?

Andrew Carnegie once stated that he owed his start in life to a game of checkers. As a youngster, his father had taken him to a friend of his to get him his first job. The gentleman in question happened to be a checker enthusiast and invited young Andrew to sit down to a game. The lad so distinguished himself by his playing ability that he got the job then and there.

Teddy Roosevelt was said to play a very good game of checkers, and I know that Thomas Edison, Harry Houdini, and Will Rogers did, for I played all of them during the years I played professionally at Luna Park, Coney Island.

Also the famous baseball pitcher, Christy Mathewson, was an even greater checker player, and was a regular visitor to the checker clubs in all the large cities. When I was just starting to learn the game I met "Matty" at the old New York Checker Club on East 42nd St., N. Y. C. His generous coaching in the tricks and traps of the game gave me my first start towards championship honors, but now we are getting a bit off our regular answers. Perhaps you might give me the next question that comes to your mind.

Assuming I have learned the rules and general principles and that I am alert to the weaknesses of my opponent, how may I escape traps which he will set for me, and in return, lay some for him?

After learning the general principles of the game, the next important step is to familiarize yourself with the various skirmish tactics. This involves learning the various traps and deceptive shots. By learning how to lay these shots and traps, you will also learn how to recognize them when they are set for you.

So I may understand exactly what a trick shot or trap is, suppose you explain to me the simplest trick shot which you know.

In order to get a clear picture of this, let's remove all the other checkers from the board.

Now, let us place checkers on the squares shown in the following diagram.

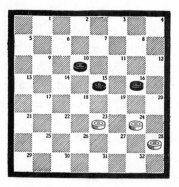

DIAG. 6. The "Two-for-One" shot. White to move and win. White wins by 24-19, 15-24, 28-12.

Now, how would you apply a shot like this in a game, and suppose my opponent catches me in a trap of this

*kind, do I have to jump or can I allow my opponent to
pick up my man instead?*

If you are caught in a shot of this kind, you *have* to jump.
The only choice is where you catch your opponent in the shot,
and if he fails to jump, *you* can either pick up his checker
(called "Huffing") *or* you can compel him to jump. (See
Law No. 13.)

The following illustration shows how the "Two-for-One"
shot just detailed can be used in a game.

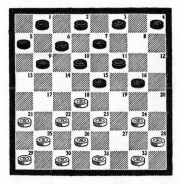

DIAG. 7. The "Two-for-One" in actual play. White moves and
wins by 24-19, 15-24, 28-12.

In the Diagram just shown the identical "Two-for-One"
shot shown on Diagram 6 is depicted as it appears in a game
surrounded by other pieces.

Are there many such trick shots available?

Yes, there are any number of trick shots and traps that come
up during a game. These shots will be shown in detail in the
next chapter.

I've often heard it said that if you retain your entire king row your opponent cannot break through. Is this true?

Decidedly not! To try and retain your entire King Row means that you are trying to fight your battle with only eight checkers, your front line four men and your secondary four men. If your opponent brings out two men from his King Row, he has an attacking force of ten men against your eight, and will soon overcome your smaller force.

Only *two men* should be retained in the King Row; a man on square 1, and a man on square 3 for Blacks. With Whites, a checker on 32 and one on 30 gives the regular King Row protection.

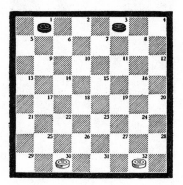

DIAG. 8. The Standard King Row defense.

How can your opponent break through this two-man King Row defense?

The only way that your opponent can enter the King Row through this defense is by forming what is known as a "Bridge Position."

To form a Bridge position, a man must first be posted

on either square 10 or square 12, which forms a bridge for a checker on square 11 to move into the King Row.

If you had your Bridge position with the Whites, Black would have to occupy either square 21 or 23, to form his bridge to enable another of his men on 24 to run through into the King Row, see Diagram 8A, which shows both players with a bridge position on opposite sides of the board.

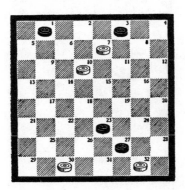

DIAG. 8A. The "Bridge" Position.

I understand a checker player must look several moves ahead in a game. Is this necessary, and how long does it take to acquire this ability?

Expert checker players do look a number of moves ahead in a game. This ability will be acquired by the student after he masters the principles of the game. After you have learned to locate your proper move you will find that you can also discover the probable reply of your opponent. In looking ahead in this manner you can see and avoid dangerous shots and traps.

I wonder if you could show me an illustration of this system of looking ahead.

In the following set-up shown on Diagram 9, White apparently has an opportunity of squeezing Black's man on square 14 by moving from 22 to 17; however, the old slogan "look before you leap" applies very forcibly here.

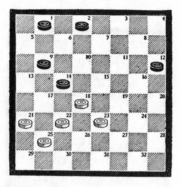

DIAG. 9. Look before you squeeze! White to move.

The novice might hurriedly push in 22 to 17 in this setting, without seeing the consequences. A look ahead will show you that if White makes the 22 to 17 move, Black simply slides his checker from 2 to 6, and after White jumps 17 to 10, Black jumps three White checkers with his piece on square 6. White's correct play was down the center of the board, namely 18 to 15. After White makes this move, Black is forced to support his checker on square 14 by playing 1 to 5. Now if White squeezes 22-17 Black can exchange 14 to 18.

Is it true that if I lose one man or even two men, that the tide of battle has turned too greatly against me, and that further fight is useless?

No. One checker behind, or even two is not always a hopeless situation. The best policy is to play your hardest right until the end of the game. It is always possible that your adversary may become careless and commit some oversight. Even the foremost players have been known to do this on certain occasions.

Suppose I am reduced to one King, which I have located in the double corner and my opponent has a King in the other double corner; is it a draw? When else is it a draw?

One King against one King, when both can reach a double corner for safety is a Drawn game. There are many forms of Drawn games, some occurring even with one King against two. The diagram below shows an ending of this kind. Black has two Kings to White's one, yet is unable to win.

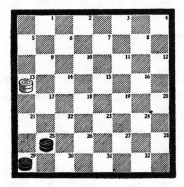

DIAG. 10.   One King draws against two. White to move and draw.

White's star play is to come after Black rather than retreat. White moves 13-17, and gains a draw position. Black can only play 25-21 or 25-30. In either case White moves 17 to 22, and as long as he keeps control of squares 26 and 22 or

17 and 22, Black is unable to release his two Kings and must agree to a draw.

Another similar setting of this idea is: Black King on 21, Black Single man on 13. White King on square 26. White to Move and Draw. Here again White forces a stalemate by moving 26-22. Black's only move is 21-17, and White plays 22-18 and blocks the escape of the Black King. Black cannot move his single man because his King is blocking it, and has only one move left for his King, which is to move back from 17-21. White must hold the grip to draw and returns to square 22, and as long as White keeps his hold on squares 22, and 18, the game must be relinquished as a Draw. The student must bear in mind that this position can also come up in the same way on the opposite side of the board.

> *Suppose I had one King in the double corner and my opponent had two. Have I lost the game, or can I hope to continue to a draw—in other words, Mr. Hopper, when is the game a draw?*

Two Kings can win against one in the Double Corner, still it is good sportsmanship to play the game out to the finish, likewise as I have mentioned there is always a small chance that your opponent might make some oversight and allow you to draw. The following shows an instance of this kind.

White has his one King in the Double Corner on square 32, while Black has Kings on 19 and 22. White instead of resigning the game moves his King out to square 27. Now Black carelessly plays 22 to 26, and White gets what is known in checker circles as the "Breeches." He moves in between the two Black kings by going from 27-23, and gains one of Black's Kings on the next move. Study this simple maneuver over for it crops up often among beginners. The following diagram shows another setting of the same idea.

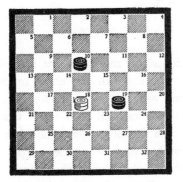

Diag. 11. The "Breeches" White to move and draw.

Here, White gets the "breeches" by moving 18-15. Amateurs seem to fall into this regularly, but you can seldom get a good player to fall for this old chestnut.

A *Draw Game* is one where neither opponent can gain any appreciable advantage over the other. It can occur with an ending of two against two, three against three, and in many ways where one opponent is a checker ahead. Many of these draw situations are shown in the chapter on End Play.

Suppose your opponent will not agree to a drawn game?

There is a special rule covering this point wherein your opponent, when notified by you through his repeating the same moves, must show an advantage in forty moves or relinquish the game as a draw. (See Standard Laws of Checkers, on page 103.)

....

CHAPTER TWO

WHAT ARE THE EXPERTS' SHOTS AND TRAPS?

The experts' shots and traps are best illustrated in a graded manner, starting with the various forms of the simple 2 for 1 shot and working on up to the 4 for 3, slip stroke, In-and-Out Combination, and other more advanced strategies. After learning each shot or trap, you should reverse the board so that you can recognize the strategy from the standpoint of your opponent. In this way, you will learn to avoid falling into the same pitfall yourself. These shots and traps compose about sixty per cent of checker ability. Once learned, you will find you can win game after game from average players without any difficulty.

We have already acquainted you with one form of the elementary "two for one" shot. We will now show another form of this same strategy.

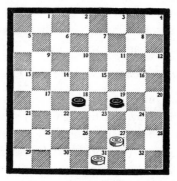

DIAG. 12. White to move and win. White wins by moving from 27 to 23.

Still other forms of this "two for one" are the following:

> Black men on 17, 18, 19
> White men on 25, 26, 29
> > White to move and win.

The solution is for white to play 25-22, and then 18-25, 29-13. Another form of the "two for one" would be set up this way:

> Black men on 10, 12, 14
> White men on 28, 24, 19
> > White to move and win.
> Solution: 19-16, 12-19, 24-6

Now to test yourself. See if you can solve the following one yourself. It is a regular "two for one" based on the similar idea to those already shown.

> Black men on 11, 15, 18
> White men on 17, 25, 26
> > Black to move and win.

The next pitfalls that the tyro usually runs up against are the three-for-one and the three-for-two shots, and we give an example of each, advising the reader to try and solve these without referring to the solution as they are based on the same idea as the "two for one" already explained. In this problem, you are playing the black checkers, so you should reverse the board so the low numbers are in front of you.

By examining the problems from both sides of the board, you will learn to detect these pitfalls when they are played on you in a game.

In Diagram 13 it is Black's turn to play and it will be found he can, by giving one man, take three in return. The

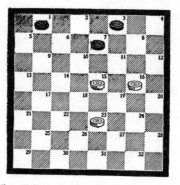

DIAG. 13. The "Three-for-One" Black to move and win.

proper move is 7 to 11, and no matter which way White jumps, Black takes three.

In Diagram 14 the same idea is shown in the three for

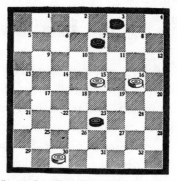

DIAG. 14. The "Three-for-Two" Black to move and win.

two. Here Black should first give away the man on 23 by moving 23 to 26; then the position is the same as Diagram 13,

which is won by moving 7 to 11. As there are several other
ways of getting three for one and three for two, we illustrate
two more of them. See if you can solve them first, as it gives
practice that is most valuable.

While these are but the elementary shots of checkers, the
beginner, nevertheless, must learn them thoroughly, and it
would be well to reverse the board on each position and view
it from the opponent's side. In this way you not only learn
how to execute it on your opponent, but how to keep from
falling into it as well.

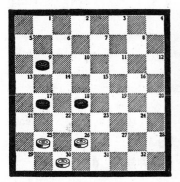

DIAG. 15. White to move and   DIAG. 16. White to move and
         win.   win.

In Diagram 15 the obvious move is 26-22 or 25-22, both
of which win, but Diagram 16 is the same idea in a more
hidden setting: here White's play is 18 to 15, Black jumping
11 to 18, then White plays 25-22 and clears the board.

THE SIDE SHOTS

Another type of shot that can be used most successfully
is the side shot, and we illustrate two of these below. It will
be noticed that the same shots come up with both colors.

Diagram 17 shows the regular side shot which can come up on various parts of the board.

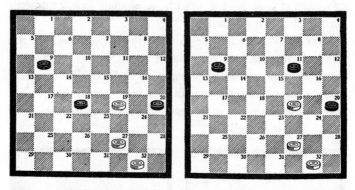

DIAG. 17. White to move and   DIAG. 18. White to move and
win.   win.

White's road to a win is by 27 to 24, Black jumping 20 to 27 and White taking three by 32 to 23 to 14 to 5. Now comes the more expert shot based on the same idea. A look at Diagram 18 will show that the position is a lot similar, only that the black man on 18 in No. 17 is now on square 11. The move to win for White here is to bring that black man back to square 18, which can be accomplished by moving the white checker on 19 to 15, forcing Black to jump 11 to 18. Here it will be seen the position is again as No. 17 and White wins by 27-24.

The reader here should study this idea well, as almost every big shot is based on this principle. For instance, the white man on 19 in No. 18 could be on square 18 and the same trick could be played by 18 to 15.

Now set the checkers up; White on 32, 28 and 18, Black on 20, 11, 9, and you have another form of the side shot almost identical. Here it will be seen White gets his shot by 18-15, then Black jumps 11 to 18 and then White plays 28-24, forcing Black to jump 20 to 27 and White crosses the board, jumping all three black checkers.

We now give the reader another one slightly different and ask him to try and solve this and the next without reverting to the solution. It can be done with a little thought and is an exercise that shows you are already improving. See Diagrams 19 and 20.

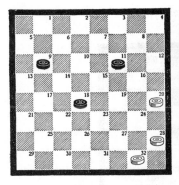 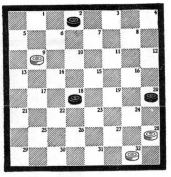

DIAG. 19. White to move and win.   DIAG. 20. White to move and win.

In Diagram 19, which I hope you have tried to solve on your own initiative, will be found a similarity to the others just given. White in this case has to have a black man on 20 to get the stroke, and this he can do by moving his white man on that square to 16, forcing Black to jump 11 to 20 and then 28-24 and the shot is complete. These maneuvers are what give the expert the big advantage over the amateur player, and the simple explanations given here should enable the reader to master them easily.

In Diagram 20 it will be found that for White to get the line-up for the side shot he must first sacrifice the man on 9, playing it 9 to 6. Black jumps and is then in position for the three-for-one side shot.

THE TRIANGLE AND DIAGONAL TWO FOR ONE

While these tricks come up with either color, we will set these up for the Blacks to win, so first reverse your board so that the low numbers are nearest you.

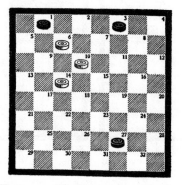

Diag. 21. Black to move and win.

In Diagram 21 we have the triangle shot, a trick which catches an amateur many times. Black might easily overlook this opportunity by plunging in for a king with the man on 27; but the move to settle things is 3 to 7, White jumping the man for a king while Black jumps two men from 1 to 10 to 17.

Diagram 22 shows part of a sister plot to No. 21; that is, both of them come up a lot in like positions. Here again as in No. 21 Black should not hurry for a king as 3 to 7 wins immediately.

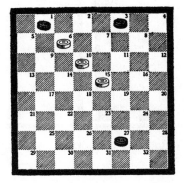

DIAG. 22.   Black to move and win.

Now let us go one step further in these types of combinations. Place black men on 1, 3, and 14. White has men on 10, 6, 23, 22, a man ahead, and it looks like an easy win for him. Black, however, plays a startling trick by moving 14 to 18 followed by 3 to 7. Try it out.

THE DOUBLE SHOT, SACRIFICING TWO AT ONCE FOR THREE, ET CETERA

White wins in Diagrams 23 and 24 by moving the man on square 19. Look at it carefully from both sides of the board.

Another example of this form of stroke is: White men on 30, 26, 18, 13. Black men 4, 5, 8, 16. White to play. Study it out and see if you can solve it. White gives away two to jump three of Black's men.

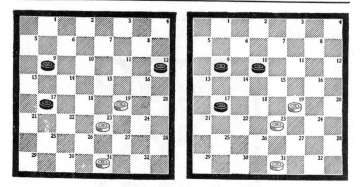

DIAG. 23. White to move and win.

DIAG. 24. White to move and win.

If you have solved this your playing has improved greatly, as this is the type of trap that the uninitiated is caught in frequently. The move to win for White, as you may have guessed, is 13 to 9, allowing Black to jump the two men from 5 to 23. White then completes the exchange by a triple jump from 26 to 3.

Now reset the same position and take the white man off 13; instead place a white king on 6. Here you have another form of the same double shot; White pushing his king to square 9, forcing Black to jump to 23 and White winning as before.

THE SLIP STROKE

Here's one for our rising checker star that looks complicated, but once the idea is learned, you sure can put it over many times on your opponents. Five to five, even pieces, but White can end the game in a few seconds. See Diagram 25. White moves 27 to 23, Black jumping into 27. White now moves 18 to 15, Black jumping 11 to 18, White retaliating 23 to 14, then Black jumping again from 9 to 18, and White puts

DIAG. 25. White to move and win.

the finishing touches on by hopping from 32 to 14—and the game is over.

DIAG. 26. White to move and win.

These are the tricks that give the spectators a thrill. The same shot can come up on other parts of the board in similar fashion. For instance No. 26 is another White win. Playing

22-18 starts things moving for Black who jumps 13-22. Now White goes from 15 to 10. Black jumps again 6 to 15. White follows with a jump 18 to 11 and Black goes 8 to 15. It is now White's grand slam as he skips over from 25 to 11, which wins the game for him as Black has only two moves left with the free man on 5 and White's man on 29 comes up and blocks him.

Still another form of the slip shot is black men on 1, 5, 10, and 15. White men on 13, 22, 24 and 28. Black in this instance is to move and win. If you can't solve it, the winning moves are 5 to 9, 13 to 6, 15-18, 22-15, 10-19, 24-15, 1 to 19 and the game is over.

DIAG. 27. White to move and win.

Another very exciting form of the slip shot is shown on the Diagram herewith. In this setting, White although a checker down can score a brilliant win. See if you can solve it, that's where the fun comes in, and that's how you can tell if you are improving.

This one is a trifle harder than the others and may keep you guessing a while. The solution is: White moves 27 to 24.

Black jumps 20 to 27, then 19 to 15, 10 to 26 and the white king captures 4 black men, blocks the remaining black single checker and wins.

If you missed solving the last one, try your hand at this one; it's almost identical with the last one, only it is on the other side of the board.

DIAG. 28. White to move and win.

These shots come up frequently in games and you have to be on the watch for them. Study these combinations carefully, first examining them before the first move is made, then look at the position after White sacrifices the first man and is ready for the final blow. In this way, the mechanics of the play will unfold themselves and you will learn the principles of this play, rather than a memory picture of the individual stroke itself.

THE IN-AND-OUT SHOT

And here comes the real fireworks, the kind that makes your opponent gasp with astonishment. Look it over first and

see how hopeless White's game appears and yet—it's a fact—
White is to move and win.

One move sets the spark to the powder and then White
just annihilates this black army. Well, if you can't solve it,
here it is. White turns the tables by moving 30 to 26, allowing
the black checker on 21 to jump into the king row. It is now
White's move and he pushes into square 2 with a smile, for

DIAG. 29. White to move and win.

the black king must now jump out of square 30 over the
white checker on square 26 and when he does so White
starts a series of jumps that starts at square 2 and ends at
square 18, capturing six black checkers in succession, and
wins.

In Diagram 30 another Big Bertha explosion occurs.
White winning again. The idea is the same as in No. 29 only
a little deeper. See if you can figure out the difference. It
takes three moves to win. White first must sacrifice a man
by playing 14 to 9, Black jumping to 14. Then White must
again sacrifice a man by 21 to 17. Black jumping to 21; now

the stage is set and White makes his "in-and-out" play by pushing 30 to 26, following by 6 to 2, and the climax of a six jump.

Study this idea carefully as there are many opportunities of working it in a game.

DIAG. 30. White to move and win.

Other forms of this are as follows:

White men on 30, 27, 21, 5. Black men on 6, 7, 8, 13, 16, 22. White, although two men behind, wins by an "in-and-out" shot. Set it up and try your skill at it. Another variation of this trick is as follows: White checkers on squares 31, 26. King on 16. Black checkers on 7, 8, 14, 24, 25.

Here it looks hopeless for White, as Black is heading for two kings and is two men ahead. However, White astonishes the onlookers by pushing from 31 to 27, allowing Black to jump into his king row. Then the white king goes from 16 to 12, and as the black king jumps out, White circles the board by jumping from 12 to 26 for a win.

THE KING STROKE

Now we introduce the checker fan to a play he no doubt has fallen into many times, the king stroke, which comes up in almost every game played, and if your opponent has not fallen into your previous traps, you still have this "old faithful" to rely on. Diagrams 31 and 32 show the simplest form of this, which should be reviewed carefully before studying its other features.

Diagram 31 shows the position to line up your kings to catch your adversary napping.

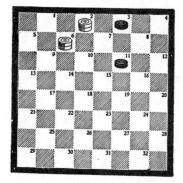 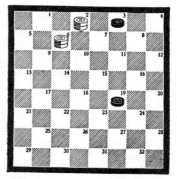

DIAG. 31. White to move and   DIAG. 32. White to move and
           win.   win.

In No. 31, it is apparent that White gets two for one by moving 2 to 7, and in No. 32 the same move, 2 to 7, gives the same result, but these are only the simple forms of this trick. We now append Diagrams 33 and 34, showing two other slightly different forms of this strategy.

In both these positions White wins by moving to square 7, giving away one man to jump the two of Black.

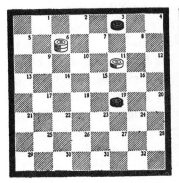

DIAG. 33. White to move and win.

DIAG. 34. White to move and win.

Now we will go a little deeper into the same idea and show you how the expert employs this stroke.

Diagrams No. 35 and No. 36 show two more White wins.

In No. 35, the expert with White would play 20 to 16, forcing Black to jump to 19, then playing 11 to 7 and clearing the board with the king.

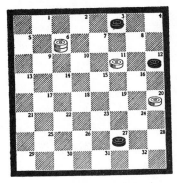

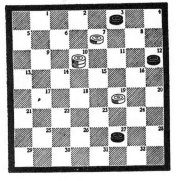

DIAG. 35. White to move and win.

DIAG. 36. White to move and win.

In No. 36 the move to win is for White to go 19 to 16, compelling Black to take 12 to 19; then, moving his king back 10 to 6, he allows the black man on 3 to jump to 10, and White sweeps across the board, taking the three blacks.

Two other forms of this problem which we hope you will try to solve by yourself are as follows: White: King on 9, men on 15 and 31. Black: King on 32, men on 2, 7. White to play and win. After this shot, we may mention, there is still one to one on the board, but White wins by the "move," which means he has the last move on his opponent. Still another forms is: White: King on 9, men on 15 and 23. Black: Men on 3, 7, 16, 24. White to move and win.

Put on your thinking caps and solve these two, and remember you have to give some away first to win.

The sacrificing of a man is one of the hardest things for the beginner to become accustomed to, yet in checkers the sacrifice is the foundation of the great majority of combination shots and strokes.

■■■

CHAPTER THREE

HOW THE BEGINNER LOSES

(Set up your boards with the white checkers facing you and follow each move as it is given.)

Now that you have become versed in the principal shots and traps, in other words the expert's bag of tricks, let us assume that you are watching over our shoulder as we play over a game and point out the faults and mistakes of the amateur.

We will assume that we have the white checkers in this game, and our opponent has the black men. As Black moves first, he makes his first move playing his checker from square 9 to square 13.

This move of Black to the side of the board is a regular fault of the beginner who seems to feel that there is more safety at the sides of the board rather than in the center. This is a fallacy, for actually a man at the side of the board is like a one-armed soldier, he can only attack in one direction. A checker in the center attacks to right and left and holds twice the potential attacking force as the man on the side.

It is now White's move and following the rule we mentioned, we play 22 to 18, Black replies by moving 10 to 14, forcing an exchange but a weak one which breaks up his Double Corner. White jumps 18 to 9 and Black replies 5 to 14.

It is now our move with the White pieces and we continue up the single corner file by playing 25-22. The purpose of this move is to prepare to attack the Black checker on 14 on the next play by going 22 to 18; however, Black's next move from 12 to 16 leaves White with the choice of two shots. He can play 23 to 18 and obtain a two-for-one shot or he can play 23 to 19 and get a similar two for one. The strongest move is 23 to 19 and we play that, causing Black to jump 16 to 23, while White jumps from 27 to 9.

Now comes a very critical situation for Black for if he goes 1 to 5, trying to recapture the man he lost, White will retaliate by a "three for one shot." We diagram the position and the student should study this trap carefully both from the Black side and from the White.

DIAG. 37. White to move and win
after Black moves 1-5.

After Black moves 1 to 5, White replies 24 to 19 and Black jumps from 5 to 14. Now study the position on your board. Black has recaptured the lost checker but in doing so, has fallen headlong into a "three for one." See if you can see the shot that White has. White's star play is to move 22 to 17. Black jumps from 13 to 22 and White jumps from 26 to 17 to 10 to 1 capturing three men and securing a King as well. To learn this trap thoroughly, the student should

play over this game several times and study the setting in
Diagram No. 37, which shows the need of looking ahead
when you are about to capture a checker. If you make it a
rule to ask yourself "Where am I going to land after I jump
the man?" and "Will it leave a shot for my opponent?"
you will find that you will be able to avoid such happenings.

Continuing the game, after White jumps into the King
Row, Black decided to eliminate the White King by exchanging men and plays from 2 to 6, White's King jumping
from 1 to 10, and Black re-jumping from 7 to 14.

This is a good exchange only Black is sadly handicapped
by being two checkers behind and every exchange made with
such a handicap increases the odds against Black. However,
the King must be eliminated, for as it stands the King is
equal in value to two Black single men.

After Black jumps from 7 to 14, White's next step is to
get a new King. Examine the position on your board and
see what man you think should be started to secure another
King. As you look at the position, you will note that Black's
weakest point is his Double Corner side of the board. Therefore you should attack in that direction. Now that you have
decided on that, which of your checkers can reach the Double
Corner King Row the quickest?

The white checkers on 29, 30 or 31 could all make the
King Row in seven moves, but which of these is the best
to move?

If you remember the rule about retaining two men in
your King Row (men on 32 and 30), you will know that
the checker on 30 should be kept in position. This leaves
either your checker on 29 or 31 to be selected as your next
move. How can you judge which of these two is the best,—
and why?

If you study the position again, you find that Black's only attack can come from the right side of the board; in other words, his single corner side as four of his five checkers are on this side of the board.

If his attack is coming from this direction, you must hold as many men on this side as possible to break it up. Therefore, your White checker on square 29 should be moved, rather than the one on 31 which will be in a position to repel the Black advance on your right.

White, therefore, moves from 29 to 25. Black has little choice of moves and can only play from 8 to 12 for if he plays 14 to 18, White immediately would start down for a King with his checker on 21.

After Black plays 8 to 12, White continues 25 to 22. Black now commits the same mistake he made earlier in the game by squeezing the White checker on square 19 (by going 11 to 16) without looking to see what can happen after making that move. Can you see what White should do at this stage? What move would you make with the White checkers? If you advance 19 to 15, Black will play 14 to 18, but by going 31 to 27, you allow him to jump your man on 19 and get two Black men in return by jumping from 27 to 18 to 9.

After this, Black's game is hopeless but we will continue the moves to the end of the game.

Black moves from 12 to 16, and White heads in for his King by 9 to 6. Black advances 16 to 19 and White crowns his man on Square 2. Black continues from 19 to 23 and White brings out his King 2 to 6 to head off the remaining two Black checkers. Black seeks to block this by going 3 to 7, but the White King changes his tactics and goes behind the checker on square 7, by moving 6 to 2. Where your opponent has several single checkers and you have a King, the policy is to try and get in front of them and head them off, or else to get behind them and pick them off one at a time. White, by getting behind the man on 7 forces that checker to run to safety.

The only safe point for the Black checker being to the side, Black moves from 7 to 11. Again, White follows up the attack on the man and advances his King from 2 to 7. Black continues 11 to 16, and White follows up 7 to 11. Now, no matter where Black moves next, his three men are completely blocked, White leaving his King on square 11 and moving either his single man on 22 or 21.

Black must give away all of his checkers and loses without getting a King.

The student should review this game several times, as it illustrates exactly how the beginner loses his games.

··

CHAPTER FOUR

WHAT ARE THE STANDARD OPENINGS OF CHECKERS?

There are 36 Standard Openings of checkers, some of the principal ones being the Single Corner, The Cross, The Kelso, The Double Corner, Old Fourteenth, The Ayrshire Lassie and Glasgow. Some of the games are derived from the movements of the pieces, the "Single Corner" being the advance down the Single Corner file. The "Double Corner" is formed by advancing your first checker from the Double Corner side of the board.

To become a good checker player is it necessary for one to learn all these openings?

"Crossboard" ability which is the experts' name for checker skill, comes from learning the principles of the game, rather than in memorizing countless opening attacks and formations. Therefore, the student need have no worry over learning several dozen different openings.

Why is the memory player at a great disadvantage?

Checker books for many years have attempted to teach checker science by asking the reader to memorize thousands of variations, as though he could become a human encyclopedia of checker moves. These attempts have scared away many a student who sought skill at the game. Actually, mathematicians have found that there are 160,000,000,000 possible moves on the checkerboard and I defy even an Einstein to memorize a small fraction of this number. As I have stated, *"You don't have to,"* for the master player can pick his correct moves, not through memory, but by figuring them out on the board during the progress of the game.

To rely solely on memory, serves to confuse the player for there are many situations on the board that resemble others yet, in which a change in position of one checker, alters everything. Also, to try and learn to play checkers by memorized moves, besides being impractical, makes the person merely an automaton. As long as your opponent follows the book moves you have memorized, the sailing is easy, but let him vary or branch off the regular line and you are entirely at sea.

> *Isn't checkers a game that depends on calculation, foresight and strategy?*

Yes, and these principles are what make a good checker player. After all, what fun would be in the game if your moves were all made mechanically from memory?

> *By learning a few standard openings, will I be able to get away to a good start in a game?*

Yes, a few standard openings well learned will equip you with a safe means of attack and defense.

> *Which standard openings should I select for my opening attacks?*

Naturally, the strongest. With the black checkers 11 to 15 is your strongest first move. With the white checkers, 23-18 is one of the best moves to reply to Black's 11-15 opening. This 23-18 move forms the Cross.

Suppose I had the Blacks, can you take me over one of these games after I have played 11-15 as my opening move?

Yes, we will start with your playing 11-15 and your opponent replying with 22 to 18, which forms what is known as the Single Corner opening. This 22-18 reply of White's is, also, a strong defense against 11-15, yet I prefer the 23-18 reply forming the Cross opening.

I will give play on the Cross opening later. Just now we will assume you have made your 11-15 move with Black and White has replied 22 to 18.

In listing the moves of the game, the black moves will be shown in the lefthand column and the white moves on the right. The various notations (a) (b) (c) etc., are used to refer to the purpose of each move and are explained in the footnotes to the game. The student in following the moves on his board should refer to the footnotes, as they occur, to find the reasons for each move.

THE SINGLE CORNER OPENING

Black moves	White moves
11-15 ....then.................22-18	
15-22 ....25-18 (a)	
8-11 (b) ....29-25 (c)	
4-8 (d) ....25-22 (e)	

(a)—25-18 is the strongest way to jump.

(b)—Moving up the Single Corner file. This file is the strongest file on which to develop and advance your men.

(c)—Advancing to back up the checker on square 18.

(d)—Black also consolidates his men.

(e)—Observe how both players have backed up their checkers.

We will now continue with the game:

Black moves		*White moves*
10-15 (f) ....then............24-20 (g)		

(f) Black occupies a key square to command the center of the board.

(g) White moves to the side to set a trap for Black. If Black moves 9-13 or 6-10, next, White would move 20-16 and after the jumps are finished, would gain a man and a King. Try this on your board to see how it works out. Then run up the game again to this point. Then continue:

Black moves		*White moves*
12-16 (h) ....then............27-24 (i)		

(h) Black blocks White's strategy and prevents White getting the shot by 20-16.

(i) Now, White has slipped and Black has a clever winning stroke known in checker circles as the "Goose Walk" or "Old Farmer." Watch how Black can secure a King from this point. The game continues:

Black moves		*White moves*
15-19 (j) ....then............24-15		
16-19 (k) 23-16		
9-14 (l) 18-9		

(j) The first move of the shot, Black must sacrifice three men before he obtains his King and recovers his men. The student should study the mechanics of this stroke.

(k) This man must be sacrificed also for if Black plays 9-14 without sacrificing the man on 16, White would get a return jump into Black's King Row.

(l) Now Black goes to town, after White jumps 18 to 9, Black hops from 11 to 25 and also wins the White checker on square 9 on the next move.

Where did White make his mistake and what should he have done?

White made his mistake when he fell into the shot at note (i). Instead of moving 27-24, his correct play was 21 to 17, which gives him an open game.

Mr. Hopper, you have mentioned the value of moving to the center of the board. Are there certain times when I can be privileged to move to the side?

Yes, there are certain situations wherein a side move is necessary. While the center of the board is the strongest, there are times when your opponent has blocked your center pathway and you must deploy pieces to the side.

Can you give me an illustration of this?

Yes, the Cross Opening explains this nicely and we will take you over one of the games. This is the opening that I suggest that you use when playing the White pieces.

THE CROSS OPENING

Black moves		White moves
11-15	..............then...............	23-18 (a)
8-11 (b)	....	27-23 (c)
4-8 (d)	....	23-19 (e)

(a) Forms the Cross Opening, so named because it cuts across the board.

(b) Black moves up to back up the man on square 15, using the center file advance.

(c) White also backs up the man advanced to square 18. Both players have moved to the center of the board, though from different directions.

(d) Black completes the three man advance and forms a strong wedge position which is ready to attack square 19 on the next move.

(e) White at this stage could move 32 to 27 also forming a wedge shaped position, but to open his King Row on square 32, although permitting of a draw, is not as strong as the move made (23 to 19) which gives White control of two key squares and, likewise, prevents Black from making his intended 15 to 19 move.

Study the position as it stands on the board. White's move 23 to 19 was made to tie up the three Black men on 8, 11, and 15. You will observe that these cannot be moved without Black losing two checkers.

DIAG. 38. Black to move.

*How should Black overcome this grip and is it not best
to strike at the hole in White's ranks formed by the open
squares 27 and 23?*

While there is a hole in White's ranks, still it is well protected by the White forces. Even so, the best move is for
Black to strike at this point, because by so doing, he will
destroy the grip White has on Key Squares 18 and 19.

How can Black make this attack?

By moving from 10 to 14. Let us make this move on our
board and note how Black removes the obstructing pieces
from the center of the board and relieves a position that was
becoming cramped.

Let us continue our game from here with Black making
10 to 14 his strongest move. Later, we will show how 9-13
loses at this stage.

Black moves	*White moves*
10-14 .... then 19-10	
14-23(f) 26-19	
7-14	

(f) If Black should jump 6 to 15, White would move
22-17 next then 15-22 or (14-23) and after the jumps are completed White gets two men on the final jump and gains a
checker.

Assuming Black has jumped correctly, we will continue
the game from this point. White plays 24-20.

Black moves	*White moves*
	24-20 (g)

(g) Here is an instance where a side move is proper and
we will explain the reasons for it. In the first place, if White

were to play 19-15, his only center move, the exchange would leave a white checker on square 15, but this checker would be away out of contact with his supporting men. Make this exchange and note the isolated position of the white checker that jumps from square 22.

Also, 24 to 20, instead of 19-15, serves to block three Black checkers formed by the triangle of Black men on squares 8, 11 and 12. This prevents Black moving from 11 to 16. After White has played 24 to 20, let us continue our game from here.

Black moves	White moves
6-10 (h) .... then ....22-17 (i)	

(h) Black moves this checker up so that it will form a bridge to allow him to release the three Black checkers on 8, 11 and 12, which are tied up by the two White checkers on 19 and 20. The Black checker moving to square 10 will now allow the Black checker on square 11 to advance to square 15.

(i) Here again is where White must revert to a side move due to the fact that he has no moves available in the center of the board.

Let us continue the game from here.

Black moves	White moves
11-15 (j) ....then..............17-13 (k)	

(j) Black has followed up his intended advance down the center. If he had played 9 to 13 at this point, White would reply 30 to 26, forcing a two for two exchange that leaves an even position. If Black played this way, White's moves following the exchange would be 26 to 23, followed by 29 to 25.

(k) The best counter attack against the 11-15 advance. While Black is weakening your Double Corner, you in return are breaking up the Double Corner side of his board.

Black moves		White moves
15-24 ....then................		13-6
2-9		28-19
8-11 (l)		30-26 (m)
14-18 (n)		

(l) Black again brings up the man on his center file to move 11 to 15 next move and attack the White man on 19.

(m) Here White plays 30 to 26 which baits a neat trap for Black.

(n) Black, seeing what looks to be a possibility of getting down to White's King Row, advances from 14 to 18. After this move is played, can you see how White strikes with a 3 for 2 shot? Black's correct draw move was to go 11 to 15 instead of 14 to 18. Let us continue after 14 to 18.

Black moves		White moves
		19-15
10-19 ....then................		26-23
18-27		31-8

Leaving White with a winning position.

If I have the Whites and play the cross against an average player, does he generally play this same variation, or had I better count on his choosing some other strategy? For, after all, I want to be prepared for anything he may do. Sometimes, I suppose, he makes a blunder that helps me?

The average player usually falls into a loss before he gets to this point. There are several very clever traps in this game, and I've won more games on these than on any others.

I wish you would show me just how the other fellow falls into these traps.

All right. Reset your men on your checkerboard with the White checkers facing you. The moves go along the lines of the game just shown—up to a certain point, and then the fireworks begin.

CROSS OPENING

Black moves		White moves
11-15 ....then.................		.23-18
8-11		.27-23
4-8		.23-19 (a)
9-14 (b)		.18-9

(a) Up to this point the game is the same as the last.

(b) This is the move that the average person makes instead of 10 to 14 as detailed in the preceding game. While 9 to 14 is a sound move, still it is not as safe as 10-14, for it leads to very tricky ground as we will show.

Continue from this point:

Black moves	White moves
5-14 (c)	.22-17 (d)

(c) This jump to the center is the strongest for Black as it puts him in control of two key squares.

(d) The position at this stage gives a clear illustration of why certain positions call for a side move. If you take back the last move 22 to 17 and examine the setting on the board, you will see that White has no opportunity to make a center move. We diagram the position:

DIAG. 39. White to move.

As you study the diagram, you will note that the only center moves White can make would be disastrous. To go 22-18 would lose a checker as Black would jump 14 to 23. Also, if White goes 26 to 23, Black would play 15 to 18, getting a two for two exchange which batters White's Double Corner and gives him an extremely weak position. Likewise, if White moves 24 to 20, and exchanges 15 to 24, 28-19, Black attacks 11 to 15 and White must play 32 to 28 to rejump after Black goes from 15 to 24. Black then follows up the attack on White's Double Corner by 8 to 11 and White can no longer protect his man on square 19, and must lose this man when Black advances 11 to 15 next move. If White goes 31-27, Black gets a 3 for 1 shot by 11 to 16.

Now reset the checkers as shown on Diagram No. 39 and continue with White making his strongest move 22-17.

At this point, you might say, "Why can't Black move 11 to 16 to attack the man on 19?" The fact is that this is the very move the average player makes and it loses immediately. See if you can discern what move White makes against it to win. The situation emphasizes the need of looking where you are going to land when you squeeze by one of your opponent's checkers. The diagram shows the position after Black's losing move 11 to 16.

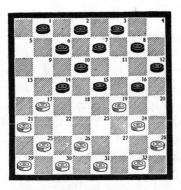

DIAG. 40. White to move.

Black's thought is that he will jump the White man on 19 next move and that White will jump back 26 to 19. If such was the case, Black's move would be all right but, unfortunately for Black, White has simply to move his checker from 31 to 27 and after Black jumps 16 to 23, it's an entirely different story as White skips three Black checkers and gains a King by jumping from 27 to 18, to 11, to 4. The student should study this situation thoroughly from both sides of the board, so that besides learning this trap, he will recognize similar ones when they come up in his games.

What was Black's correct move?

Set up the position as in Diagram No. 40 and move back the Black checker from square 16 to square 11, this was Black's losing play. Now play 15 to 18, which is Black's proper move. The game continues:

Black moves	White moves
15-18 (e)	26-22 (f)

(e) Black's best move. If Black plays 14 to 18, White would exchange 17 to 14 and occupy square 14 after the jumps and get a very strong game.

(f) This is White's best move and a very tricky one, for again if Black plays 11 to 16, White will gain a checker as follows 11-16, 22-15, 16-23, 31-27 *, 10-19, 17-10 *, 7-14, 27-9, 6-13, 24-15, and White is a man up. Also, if Black goes 1 to 6 or 2 to 6, next move White gets another shot by 15 to 10, 6-15, 21-17, 13-22, 25 to 4. The student should study this very closely. The * (star) next to certain moves means they are star plays.

Now reset your checkermen for the start of a game and play up to this point again. The moves are:

Black moves	White moves
11-15 ....then................	23-18
8-11	27-23
4-8	23-19
9-14	18-9
5-14	22-17
15-18	26-22
11-15 (g)	17-13 (h)
7-11 (i)	

(g) Black makes his strongest move. If he moves 18-23, White would play 19-15 and get a strong game.

(h) After White makes this move, Black might hastily go 14 to 17 but if he figures the situation out ahead he will see that White gets the last two jumps and gains a man thus 14-17, 21-14, 10-30, 19-10 *, 7-14, 31-15.

(i) Black's best move. The natural move is 8-11, but you will observe that 8-11 allows a "two for one" shot. White plays 24-20 against it and after Black jumps 15-24, White jumps from 22 to 8 and wins.

Now to continue the game with Black avoiding these traps by playing 7 to 11.

Black moves	*White moves*
	22-17 (j)

(j) White again must make a side move as he has no possible way to advance down the center. The move made 22-17 sets another neat trap for Black. If Black plays 11-16 at this point, White gets a neat three for two shot by playing 31-27, 16-23, 25-22, 18-25, 27-4, a neat and spectacular win.

Now reset your men and run the game up again.

Black moves	*White moves*
11-15	23-18
8-11	27-23
4-8	23-19
9-14	18-9
5-14	22-17
15-18	26-22
11-15	17-13
7-11	22-17
2-7 (k)	32-27 (l)

(k) We have shown how 11-16 loses by 31-27 followed by 25-22. This move, 2-7 is the correct play at this stage.

(l)   Baits another trap for Black. The beginner would now be inclined to play 11-16, but make that move, and then continue 27-23, 18-27, 13-9 and White has all the best of it.

What was Black's correct play at this stage?

We diagram the position at this point.

DIAG. 41. Black to move.

The correct move here is for Black to play 1-5, then White continues 30-26. Now Black must play 5 to 9 for 11-16 again gives White a shot by 27-23, 18-27, 26-22, 16-23, 22-18, 15-22, 25-2 and White wins.

Now reset the position as in Diagram No. 41 and continue, with Black playing 1-5, 30-26, 5-9, then 26-22 and now Black can play 11-16, White continues 27-23, 18-27, 22-18, 15-22 *, 25-18, 14-23, 24-20, 8-11, 31-24, 23-26, 19-15, 10-19, 24-8, ending in a Drawn game.

Now we have taken you over the regular line of the Cross

Opening, showing the various pitfalls which Black can fall a victim to. Let us play over another interesting Cross game which, also, shows an interesting win for White.

CROSS OPENING

Black moves	White moves
11-15 ....then...................23-18	
8-11 27-23	
4-8 23-19	
9-13 (a)	

(a) This move loses for Black as White blocks Black's advance and forces a neat shot. Watch how White consolidates his men and forces the three for two shot. Continue:

Black moves	White moves
....................................26-23	
6-9 30-26	
9-14 18-9	
5-14 ....32-27 (b)	
1-5 ....19-16 (c)	
12-19 23-16	
11-20 22-17	
13-22 25-4	

White wins

(b) The beginner might jump for the two for one shot by 22-17, but Black could move 1-5 and recover the man. By moving 32-27, White prepares a better shot which Black cannot avoid.

(c) Sets off the shot. Study this closely. The Diagram shows the situation.

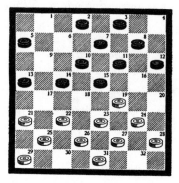

DIAG. 42. White to move and win.

Now, Mr. Hopper, you have shown me the various pit-falls that come up for Black in the "Cross Opening." Suppose you give me a résumé of the entire game with each of Black's danger points designated.

All right, I believe that this will help you to get a better idea of the cross game as a whole. In order to make this clear, I will list all the moves in one column with the notes next to them.

11-15

23-18   This move of White's forms the Cross Opening.

8-11

27-23

4-8

23-19

9-14   (10-14 is also good but 9-13 loses for Black here by 26-23, 6-9, 30-26, 9-14, 18-9, 5-14, 32-27, 1-5, 19-16)

18-9   Here the two players exchange men—first blood!

5-14

22-17

15-18   if 14-18 then 17-14 for White (if 11-16 Black loses by 31-27)

26-22

11-15   if 11-16 Black loses by 22-15, 16-23, 31-27

17-13

7-11   if 8-11 Black loses by 24-20; 14-17 also loses.

22-17

2-7   if 11-16 Black loses by 31-27, 16-23, 25-22

32-27

1-5   if 11-16, 27-23, 18-27, 13-9 White best

30-26

5-9   if 11-16 Black loses by 27-23, 18-27, 26-22, 16-23, 22-18

26-22

11-16

27-23

18-27

22-18

15-22   if 14-23 Black loses by 24-20

25-18

14-23   if 16-23, 18-15, 10-19, 17-1 White best

24-20

8-11

31-24

23-26

19-15

10-19

24-8

Drawn, although each player has seven pieces on the board.

Assuming I have the Whites at the start of a game and my opponent does not make 11-15 as his first move, what defense can I make against his other moves?

Black has six possible moves to open the game besides 11 to 15. I will list them in order with the name of the opening they form and *White's best reply to each.*

9-13 EDINBURGH OPENING

If Black moves 9 to 13, it forms the Edinburgh opening, the weakest of the Black attacks. White's best reply to 9-13 is 22-18.

9-14 DOUBLE CORNER OPENING

If Black moves 9-14, it forms the Double Corner opening. White's best reply is 22-18.

10-14 DENNY OPENING

If Black moves 10-14, White's best reply is 22-18.

10-15 KELSO OPENING

If Black moves 10-15, White's best reply is 22-18.

11-16 BRISTOL OPENING

If Black moves 11-16, White's best replies are 22-18 or 23-18.

12-16 DUNDEE OPENING

If Black moves 12-16, White can reply with 24-20 or 22-18.

....

CHAPTER FIVE

HOW CAN YOU LOCATE YOUR BEST MOVE?

Now that I have learned that my best opening move with Blacks is 11-15, and my best reply with White is 23-18, I still feel that I need help on finding my best move after the game gets going. Suppose you try me out, with a few critical situations and see how I make out.

That's a very good idea, for the ability to pick out your best move in a game is an indispensable one in playing good checkers. On the following page, I am diagraming six different checker positions. I'd like you to study each one, and see what move you would make. In each case, you have the White checkers and it is your turn to play. Write down on a paper the move that you decide on for each, then turn to the following page and check your answers. If you have solved half of them correctly, you can be sure you are well on the road to crossboard ability.

Write down your answers to each Diagram appearing on the following page, before looking at the answers on page 61.

WHAT MOVE WOULD YOU MAKE?

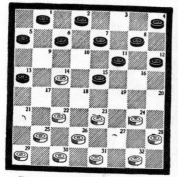

DIAG. 43. White to move.

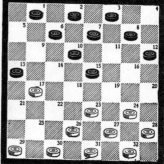

DIAG. 44. White to move.

DIAG. 45. White to move.

DIAG. 46. White to move.

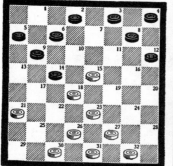

DIAG. 47. White to move.

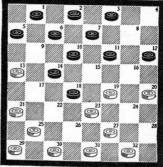

DIAG. 48. White to move.

ANSWERS TO PROBLEMS 43-48

DIAGRAM 43—White's best move is a Three-for-Two shot. He plays 14-9, Black jumps 5-14, then 23-18, 14-23, 26-3, and gains a man and has a winning position.

DIAGRAM 44—White's best move is to go 30 to 25, allowing Black to jump 13-22, while White jumps three Black men in return.

DIAGRAM 45—White could play 14-9, 5-14, 24-19, 16-23, 27-9, and gain a winning position—however White's best move is to simply play 24-20, and when Black jumps 10-17, White jumps from 20 to 4 and gains a man as well as a King.

DIAGRAM 46—In this setting, White can force the Slip Shot by playing 22-18, allowing Black to jump and then moving 14-10, 7-14, 18-9, 5-14, 27-9, and gains a winning position.

DIAGRAM 47—Here White can get a clever Three-for-Two shot by playing 15 to 11. Black jumps 8-22, and White jumps from 26 to 1 and has a winning game.

DIAGRAM 48—19 to 15 is White's best move, and nets him a three jump and a King.

That was quite a lot of fun. Now suppose you give me another group of these "move finders" and make them even harder to guess.

All right, I'll set 'em up for you, and see if you can pick them. Frankly, this is the best exercise to put you in form for trimming that fellow who took you over recently. One thing though—please don't peek ahead to find the answer, or you will spoil all the fun. Just take your time and try and guess them, by applying the principles we have already outlined. Don't use snap judgment and decide on the very first move that strikes you. Generally if you look over the situation carefully and ask yourself a few questions, you will find a better move. You have five minutes solving time on each diagram; if you can pick them in less, so much the better.—Now go to it.

Five minutes solving time on each to pick the best move.

Write down your selections for the best move for each setting on a piece of paper and then turn to the following page and see how you made out.

WHAT MOVE WOULD YOU MAKE?

Diag. 49. White to move.

Diag. 50. White to move.

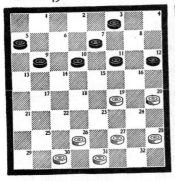

Diag. 51. White to move.

Diag. 52. White to move.

Diag. 53. White to move.

Diag. 54. White to move.

ANSWERS TO PROBLEMS 49-54

DIAGRAM 49—Shows how easy it is to miss a neat win White moves 19-16 and gives Black a big surprise. If Black jumps 12-19, then White plays 32-28, and gets a three jump on the next move.

DIAGRAM 50—The "Two-for-One" shot by 22-17 is *not* White's best move. Instead, play 15-10, 6-24, 27-4 and see what happens.

DIAGRAM 51—The magic formula here is 20-16, 11-20, 19-16, 12-19, followed by 27-24, 20-27, 31-6.

DIAGRAM 52—Did you look at 19-15? This gives you a neat shot and a winning game.

DIAGRAM 53—If you paused to consider what happens if you move 24-19, you would find it releases you from a perilous situation.

DIAGRAM 54—This one crops up often in a game. White moves 22-18, which forces 15-22. This removes the Black checker on 15, and opens the road for White to get a Two-for-Two shot next move by 19-15. White also gains the Black checker that jumped from 10-26.

Well, Mr. Hopper, I'm beginning to feel like a checker player already. Suppose you show me a few more of these that come up nearer the close of a game.

I'll be glad to do that and this training will be a very valuable help to you, for in our next chapter I will spread out a whole assortment of checker "brain teasers" that cover every type of shot, trap and stroke in checkers, also some that depend on sacrifice and power plays. It will be up to you to try and solve them by yourself—however, if you find some that are "too tough" for you, why I suppose we'll have to let you turn to the answer page for that one. Now for those other "What move would you make" endings.

Endings with 5 minute solving time. (Turn the board so that the low numbers are nearest you, in studying these settings.)

And no peeping at the answers on the next page until you have written down the moves you would make on each.

DIAG. 55. Black to move.

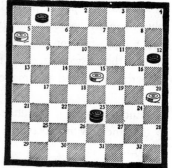

DIAG. 56. Black to move.

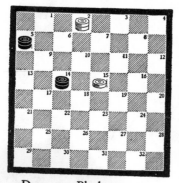

DIAG. 57. Black to move.

DIAG. 58. Black to move.

DIAG. 59. Black to move.

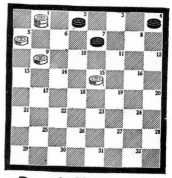

DIAG. 60. Black to move.

ANSWERS TO PROBLEMS 55-60

DIAGRAM 55—Solution: Black wins by 23-18, 14-23, 5-9, 13-6, 1-17.

DIAGRAM 56—Black wins by: 12-16, 20-11, 23-18, 15-10, 18-15, 11-7, 15-6, 7-2, 6-9, 2-7, 9-14, 7-2, 14-18, 2-7, 18-15, 7-2, 15-11.

DIAGRAM 57—Black wins by 20-24, 27-20, 7-3, 20-16.

DIAGRAM 58—Black wins by 7-10, 15-6, 4-8.

DIAGRAM 59—Black wins by 14-10, 15-6, 5-1.

DIAGRAM 60—Black wins by 11-16, 19-15, 22-18, 14-23, 16-19, 23-16, 12-10.

....

CHAPTER SIX

CHECKER BRAIN TEASERS

Fascinating Fun and Training for Your Checker Honors

Earlier in this book, Mr. Hopper, you showed me the various traps and shots of checkers. Suppose you set up some of these strategies and see if I can solve them? Perhaps you might give me some of the easier ones first and work up to the real puzzlers.

I'll do that but I'd like to ask you to bear in mind that, while most of the settings give the White checkers the opportunity to win, still the same strategy can come up with the Black checkers as well. In other words, if you learn the basic principles of the strategies, you will recognize them in play, regardless of what color the checkers you are handling. It is best to set up the positions on your numbered board rather than trying to solve them from the diagram.

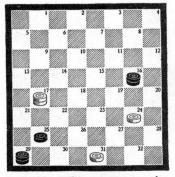

DIAG. 61. White moves to win.

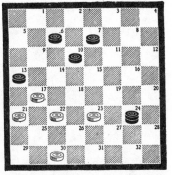

DIAG. 62. White moves to win.

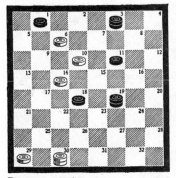

DIAG. 63. White moves to win.

DIAG. 64. White moves to win.

DIAG. 65. White moves to win.

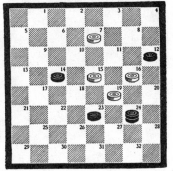

DIAG. 66. White moves to win.

DIAG. 67. White moves to win.

DIAG. 68. White moves to win.

DIAG. 69. White moves to win.

DIAG. 70. White moves to win.

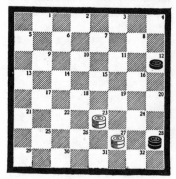

DIAG. 71. White moves to win.

DIAG. 72. White moves to win.

SOLUTIONS TO CHECKER BRAIN TEASERS

DIAGRAM 61—24-19, 16-23, 31-26, 23-30, 17-21. White wins.

DIAGRAM 62—22-18, 13-22, 23-19, 24-15, 18-2. White wins.

DIAGRAM 63—10-7, 1-17, 29-25, 3-10, 25-22. White wins.

DIAGRAM 64—11-7, 2-11, 26-23, 17-26, 27-24, 28-19, 23-14, 9-18, 30-14. White wins.

DIAGRAM 65—26-22, 18-25, 21-17, 14-21, 19-16, 12-26, 27-31. White wins.

DIAGRAM 66—15-10, 24-6, 7-2, 12-19, 2-27. White wins.

DIAGRAM 67—28-24, 20-27, 26-22, 17-19, 32-5. White wins.

DIAGRAM 68—32-27, 23-32, 2-7, 11-9, 5-23. White wins.

DIAGRAM 69—19-16, 11-27, 18-15, 10-26, 32-5. White wins.

DIAGRAM 70—22-17, 21-25, 17-21(A), 10-14 (B), 18-9, 25-30, 21-25(C), 30-21, 9-6, 21-17, 6-2, 17-14, 2-7. White wins.

> (A) If 17-13 here, Black draws by 10-14, 18-9, 25-30, 13-17, 30-26, 17-14, 26-23. Drawn.
>
> (B) Best. If 25-30, White plays 18-14, 10-17, 21-14 and wins.
>
> (C) A super move, and only one to win. If 9-6, then 30-26, 6-2, 26-23. Drawn.

DIAGRAM 71—27-32, 28-24, 23-18, 24-28(A), 18-15, 28-24, 32-28, 24-27, 15-18, 12-16, 28-32, 27-24, 18-15, 24-28, 15-11, 16-19, 32-27, 28-32, 27-31, 19-23, 11-15, 32-28, 15-19. White wins.

(A) If 12-16 here, then continue: 12-16, 18-15, 16-20, 15-18, 24-19, 32-28, 19-16, 18-23, 16-11, 23-19, 11-8, 28-32, 8-11, 32-27, 11-8, 27-23, 8-3, 23-18, 3-8, 18-15. White wins.

DIAGRAM 72—5-9, 1-5, 9-13, 5-1, 11-15, 2-6, 10-14, 6-2, 14-9, 1-6, 9-5, 6-1, 15-10, 2-6, 10-7, 3-10, 5-9. White wins.

In this last problem the Move plays a very important part. If it were Black's move first the game would be a Draw.

■■■

CHAPTER SEVEN

THE END GAME

As a game comes to a close, Mr. Hopper, can a player relax? I have often seen players sit back near the finish of a game and say, "Now I have less men to worry about, I guess I can afford to take it easy."

Because there are less men on the board is no sign that you can "take it easy." Many games are won and lost during the ending stages. While there are fewer pieces on the board, the importance of each piece becomes greater and one innocent looking move may change a victory to a defeat.

What are the main points to watch out for at the closing stages of the game?

First, see that you get your single men out of danger from any King that your adversary may secure and, secondly, endeavor to advance these single men towards your King Row in order that your opponent may not be able to block one or more of them with his King. One King can block two single checkers on the side of the board and where the ending is three to three, such an advantage would win. The one King pinning the two single men would leave two Kings which could defeat your opponent's single King.

What is the meaning of "the move" in checkers and what part does it play in games?

The *move* in checkers means—having the *last move*. When each player has a few checkers left and are advancing towards each other, generally the one with the last move or MOVE wins. THIS SYSTEM of the move plays an important part in experts' games. They can calculate who will have the MOVE several plays ahead and play accordingly.

If your adversary has this "move" or last move how can you change it in your favor?

An ordinary exchange of "one for one" will take the move away from your opponent and give it to you.

How can you tell if you have the move?

This can best be explained by the aid of diagrams. Set up the position shown in Diagram 73.

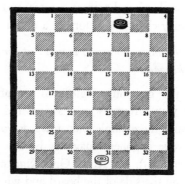

DIAG. 73. White to move and win.

Suppose you were playing the Whites and you headed directly for the Black checker, you would win because you had the last move: make the plays on your board. White 31-27—then—Black 3-7.

White moves	Black moves
27-23	7-10
23-18	White wins

No matter how Black played from this position, White can always block him because he has the "MOVE."

If the White checker in Diagram 73 were on Square 27 and it was White's move, the situation would be the reverse as Black would then have the last move or "MOVE" and win.

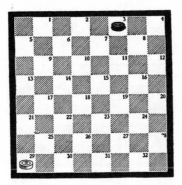

DIAG. 74. It is Black's move, and as he has the "Move," he can win.

How can you figure out who has the move in any given position?

The system of finding who has the "MOVE" is a very interesting one and will well reward anyone for learning it for you can tell at any point of the game whether or not you will have the last move.

The following diagram shows a checkerboard with 8 rows of perpendicular lines, one set of lines are dotted, the other lines heavy and unbroken. The heavy, unbroken lines you must remember as "your system," while the dotted lines are your "opponent's system."

It is not difficult to fix this in your mind if you simply

note that your system starts at each of your King Row squares and runs straight across the board.

Square 32 is the first playing square on your right in your King Row. Starting at this Square and following the black line across the board, you cross playing Squares 32, 24, 16 and 8. The next square in your King Row is 31 and each of the squares directly in line with 31, are 23, 15 and 7. The same applies for the other two squares of your King Row.

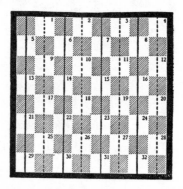

DIAG. 74A. The system of the "MOVE."

In other words, every Black playing square directly in line with your King Row squares are in "your" system. These squares are all crossed by the solid line in the diagram.

Now that you know the squares in your system, you are in a position to tell at any time in a game who will have the last move.

When it is your turn to play you look at the board and count all the checkers, *both yours and opponent's,* that are on squares in your system. If the number is odd, you have the "MOVE," if it is even your opponent has the "MOVE."

To illustrate this, set up Black single checkers on squares

7 and 17, and set up White single men on Square 30 and 26.

It being your move with White, you want to find if you have the "MOVE" or last move, so you start to count the checkers in your system. Remember, you count all the checkers in your system, both your opponent's and your own. Placing your finger on the first square in your King Row (square 32) you run it straight across the board. There are no checkers on this first row in your system, so you move to the next square in your King Row, square 31, and again running your finger across the board, you come to your opponent's checker on square 7. You count this ONE. Now, going to the next row in your system, you arrive at square 30, which is the only checker on this row. This you count with the one already counted on square 7, which makes a total of TWO. There being no checkers on the last row in your system starting at square 29, you find a total of two checkers in your system. Two being an even number, your opponent has the "MOVE" or last move, and if you move, you will find he will block your checkers—thus White moves 26-23, Black plays 17-22, White 23-19, Black 7-11 and wins. Remember, that you always calculate who has the move when it is your turn to play.

Assuming my opponent has the "move" in the position just given, how can I change the "move" so that he will be unable to block me and win?

That's very simple. An ordinary exchange of one for one, always changes the "MOVE." For instance, reset the same position. Black men on 7 and 17, White on 26 and 30. As it stands your opponent has the "MOVE" and can block your pieces, but instead of moving towards him, simply exchange 26 to 22; he jumps 17 to 26 and you rejump 30 to 23. This changes the move and instead of him blocking you, you have the "MOVE" and can block his checker and win—thus 7 to 10, 23-18 and White wins.

Say! That's a wonderful system and you say it works no matter how many men there are on the board?

Yes, providing you both have the same amount of men. There are games wherein the pieces become deadlocked in a block when there are still 12 checkers on each side. In such a case, the player having the "MOVE" will know he is going to win many moves ahead.

Now that I have learned the system of finding if I have the move, is it necessary for me to figure this out all through the game?

No, it is not, only when the game gets into the finishing stages, say 4 to 4 or 3 to 3, then it is important to find whether you or your opponent has the "MOVE." If your opponent has the move, you can regain it by a "one for one" exchange, but remember you will then have to avoid another "one for one" exchange as that would again return the move to your opponent.

If a game appears to be getting into a deadlock in the early stages, you should check up to see if you have the "move," and, if so, try and maintain it. Many games are won and lost on the ending by the finesse of the "MOVE."

....

CHAPTER EIGHT

SOME OPENING "BLITZKRIEGS"

Mr. Hopper, is there such a thing as a Blitzkrieg in checkers, a game where suddenly, by a swift and unexpected stroke, your opponent completely annihilates your forces?

Yes, there are just such situations in checkers which might be likened to a Blitzkrieg. There are certain games in which spectacular strokes follow one upon another, sweeping the checkers from the board and practically annihilating your game.

I wish you would show me a few of these spectacular grandstand plays; just in case—

Set up your checkerboard for the start of a game with the White checkers facing you. The first of these super-strokes that I will show you happens after only a few moves are made. It is known by experts as the "Canalejas" stroke and dates back to 1500.

Black moves		White moves
11-16	................then................	.23-18
16-20	....	.24-19
8-11 (a)	....	

(a) The losing move and White applies the heat full force. Just watch him blast his way into Black's King Row— but first, look it over and see what move you would make with White's. The Blitzkrieg opens with a sacrifice and runs as follows. Continue with White's move.

Black moves		White moves
		19-15
10-19	....	18-14
9-18	....	22-8
4-11	....	27-24 (b)
20-27	....	31-8

(b) The second bomb explodes and leaves Black with a hopeless game.

That's a good one for my bag of checker tricks. I'm sure I will be able to get that one on some of my opponents. Now let's see another.

This time, Black will be the purveyor of checker destruction and again it all happens in a few moves. Turn the board so that the Black checkers are facing you.

Black moves		White moves
10-14	................then................	23-19
11-16	....	26-23
9-13	....	24-20
14-17 (a)	....	21-14 (b)

(a) There's dynamite in this one and there's no escape for White after the 24-20 move.

(b) If 20-11 Black jumps 17-26, then 31-22, 8-31 Black wins. Continue:

Black moves		White moves
6-10 (c)	................then................	20-11
10-26 (d)	....	31-22
8-31 Black wins		

(c) forces the shot.

(d) Note how this jump opens the way for the following Black jump to the White's King Row.

Mr. Hopper, I've heard checker experts refer to the "big shot in the 'Old Fourteenth.'" Could you show me this famous play?

Before I show you this big stroke, I might explain that the "Old Fourteenth" is one of the old time openings of checkers. This was the 14th game in Sturges' book, published in 1800. It was popular for many years with checker experts, probably due to its famous stroke. This stroke comes up as follows:

Black moves		White moves
11-15	. . . . then.	23-19
8-11	. . . .	22-17
4-8 (a)	. . . .	17-13
15-18	. . . .	24-20
11-15	. . . .	28-24
8-11	. . . .	26-23
9-14	. . . .	31-26
6-9	. . . .	13-6
2-9	. . . .	26-22
9-13 (b)	. . . .	20-16 (c)
11-20	. . . .	22-17
13-22	. . . .	21-17
14-21	. . . .	23-14
10-17	. . . .	25-2
		White wins

(a) Forms the Old Fourteenth Opening. Note the Center file advance of Black and how his men are consolidated.

(b) Black's losing move. Either 3-8 or 1-6 will draw for Black.

(c) The Fireworks begin. This stroke exemplifies the beautiful combinations that can arise in checkers.

These Blitzkriegs are quite exciting. I wonder if you can show me another one in which Black gets the upper hand.

Another clever stroke occurs in what is known as the "Slip Cross" opening. Black defending against the Regular Cross Opening takes a very tricky line known among experts as the "Slip Cross," so named by the novel slip move made by Black at his third move. The game goes as follows:

Black moves		White moves
11-15	...............then...............	23-18
8-11	....	27-23
11-16 (a)	....	18-11

(a) Forms the Slip Cross Opening. Black's slip from 11 to 16 loses a man but he gets it back after his next move.

The game continues:

Black moves		White moves
16-20	...............then...............	24-19 (b)
7-16	....	22-18
4-8	....	25-22
8-11	....	29-25 (c)
10-14	....	19-15
3-8	....	22-17 (d)
20-24 (e)	....	28-19
16-20	....	17-10
9-14	....	18-9
11-27	....	31-24
20-27	....	32-23
6-24 Black wins		

(b) This is White's best defense against the Slip Cross.

(c) 22-17 is a much safer and stronger line for White.

(d) The loser for White. White's correct move here is 31-27.

(e) This lights the fuse for a big series of checker explosions.

Mr. Hopper, what is the biggest stroke of this kind?

Why, there is a stroke that comes up in the "Ayrshire Lassie" opening which takes 18 pieces off the board. It starts with each player having 12 checkers, but before the smoke of battle clears away, there are only three checkers of each player left on the board. However, the heavy exchange of blows ends in a draw rather than a win for either player.

The position arises as follows:

Black moves		*White moves*
11-15 ....then..............		24-20 (a)

(a) Forms the Ayrshire Lassie Opening. The title of the opening, like many others in checkers, having its origin in England where "checkers" is known as "Draughts."

The game continues:

Black moves		*White moves*
8-11 ....then..............		28-24
4-8		23-19
9-14		22-17
5-9		26-23
9-13 (a)		20-16
11-20 (b)		30-26
13-22		25-4
14-18 (c)		23-14
10-17		21-14
3-8 (d)		4-11
7-30		14-10 (e)
6-15		31-26
30-23		27-11
20-27		32-23

(a) The fun begins.

(b) If Black jumps 13-22 first, he loses by 25-9, 6-13, 30-25, 11-20, 21-17, 13-22, 25-4.

(c) Now Black decides to take a fall out of White. Study this situation closely as it comes up in different games.

(d) Black puts over his stroke.

(e) White still has one more up his sleeve and after it's over, the board is almost cleared.

■■■

CHAPTER NINE

WAYS TO DRAW WITH A
MAN DOWN

*Ofttimes in a game, I end up with one man down. What
is the best thing to do in a case of this kind? In other
words, how can I put up the best fight in a situation of
this kind?*

That's a very good question, for even with a man down, you
can often put up such stiff resistance that your opponent, if
not expertly qualified, may be unable to win. With one King
against two Kings, unless you are fortunate to secure the
draw position shown on Page 15 your chances are very slim.
However, the best haven of refuge for your one King is in
either of the Double Corners. Your opponent can rout you
out in a few correctly made moves, but an amateur may let
you escape again to the other Double Corner. The proper way
to win with two Kings against one in the Double Corner is
as follows:

Place White King in square 32 and Black Kings on 23
and 31. It is White's move and he plays 32 to 28. Black moves
31 to 27 and White returns from 28 to 32. Black now moves
27 to 24 and White is forced from 32 to 28. Black then plays 23
to 19 and when White moves from 28 to 32, advances his
King on 24 into square 28. This compels White to move out
of the Double Corner and his only move is 32 to 27.

Black now moves behind the man on 27 by playing 28 to
32. White retreats to square 31 and here is where the amateur
usually goes wrong. Black's proper move now is from 19 to

15 and not 19 to 23, which allows White to squeeze 31 to 27 and possibly escape to the other Double Corner. After 19-15, White must play 31 to 26. Now Black comes after him by moving 15 to 18 and when White retreats 26 to 31, Black plays 18 to 22 and has him cornered.

Supposing I have two Kings and my opponent has three, what tactics should I resort to then?

With two Kings against three, you can put up a very stiff resistance. In fact, if you make the best moves, it will take an expert to beat you.

The best and strongest defense is to try and get one of your Kings in each Double Corner. There is only one way to beat this and only the very best players know how to do it. In fact, you will find players far better than average who will claim that this is a regular draw position and can't be beaten.

If your opponent starts to try and drive out either of your Kings from either double corner, you can feel assured that the game will end in a Draw, for no matter how he attacks one corner, as soon as things become too hot in that corner, you simply move the King in the other double corner.

Is there anything that I must watch out for while this is going on?

Yes, a very important thing and that is, you must watch out that your opponent cannot get an exchange of one for one, for if he does, it will leave him with 2 Kings to your one, which as I have shown you is a simple win.

What are the ways that my opponent might trap me into a swap or exchange?

Suppose you had a White King on square 32, and your other White King on square 5. We will assume your opponent does

not know the secret of winning and attempts to concentrate
his attack on your King on square 5. Suppose he lined up his
Kings, three Kings on squares 9, 14 and 17. In this position,
you would have to move your King on square 32, for if you
played 5 to 1, he could exchange next move by 9 to 6, 1 to 10,
14 to 7.

Again, suppose you have your Kings on 5 and 32 and he
has his three Kings on 6, 10 and 3. Here again, if you move
5 to 1, he can play 10 to 7, and force you to jump 1 to 10,
while he rejumps 7 to 14.

Still again, with your Kings on 5 and 32, and his Kings
on 6, 10 and 19, you must avoid moving 5 to 1. If you do, he
would simply move 10 to 15 and again get the swap needed
to win.

By careful play you can always avoid these exchanges.
Take for instance the following situation: White Kings on
5 and 27. Black Kings on 6, 11 and 19. Once more, if you
exercise caution and ask yourself what will happen if you
play 5-1, you will see that he can reply with 11 to 15 and get
his exchange.

*Now, assuming I have learned to play cautiously and
avoid these exchanges, what then is the secret way that
this position can be beaten?*

The one *and only* way that this position can be beaten is as
follows: Place White Kings on squares 24 and 6 and play
Black Kings on 14, 18 and 23. This is the first stage of winning this troublesome position. To attack either single White
King individually is wasted motion and can never win unless,
as I mentioned, you make an oversight and allow an exchange.

For the three Kings to win, they must first form this
lineup in the center of the board. The play that follows shows

how Black must make several moves in their proper order to secure the win.

The Diagram shows the position.

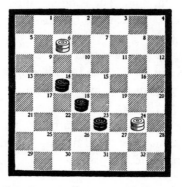

DIAG. 75. A "jinx" to the beginner. Black to move and win.

Here's how Black wins:

Black moves	White moves
18-15 ....then................. 6-1 (a)	
14-9 (b) ....24-28 (c)	
* 23-19 (d) 1-5	
* 9-6 (e) ....28-32 (f)	
* 19-24 5-1	
* 24-19 ....Black wins	

If 28-32, instead of 5-1 at White's last move, Black simply goes 6 to 10 and gets the swap needed to win.

(a) White is forced to retreat to one of the Double Corners.

(b) Black follows the retreating King and by posting his King on 9, prevents the White King from moving 1 to 5, for if this move is made, Black plays 15-18 and gets an exchange.

(c) The only move White can make.

(d) Note how this move compels White to move the

King on square one, for Black threatens to exchange by 9 to 6 on the next move.

(e) Again Black must make this Star move to hold his grip.

(f) If White plays 5 to 1 instead, Black replies with 6 to 10 and gets an exchange next move by 19-24 or 10 to 6.

Supposing that in a "three to two" ending it so happens that I cannot maneuver my two Kings to each Double Corner, what then is my next best plan?

The next best plan is to move your two Kings to either Double Corner, and again watch that your opponent does not force an exchange of one for one. There are several ways he may get an exchange by your oversight, but there is actually only one way he can force an exchange if you play correctly.

If your opponent does not know this one way to win, you can get a Drawn game.

The following position shows how you have retreated to one of the Double Corners with your two Kings and Black starts to crowd you with his three Kings.

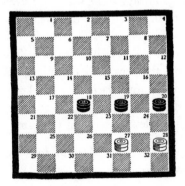

DIAG. 76. Black to move and win.

If Black plays 19-23, you can be sure he does not know how to win this ending. You reply 28-32 and if Black is not careful and plays 23-26, you would get a 2 for 1 shot by 27-24, 20-27, 32-14 and draw. Black's star moves from the Diagram are as follows:

Black moves		White moves
18-15	................then	28-32
19-24 *		27-31
24-28 * (a)		31-27
15-19 (b)		27-31
20-24 (c)		32-27 (d)
28-32 *(e)		27-20
19-24		20-27
32-23 Black wins		

(a) The player with the three should endeavor to get one King posted in the Double Corner.

(b) This is the winning play, although it offers a two for one shot by 27-24, 20-27, 32-16. However, it still wins for Black as he moves out 28-24 and blocks the King on 16. Amateurs with the 3 Kings always seem wary and avoid allowing this two for one with the result that they generally give the game up as a Draw.

(c) The Key to the whole situation. This is the clever dodge that gains the win, and the student should study it closely. Black to win must sacrifice a checker.

(d) Only move. If 31-26, then 19-23.

(e) Shows the clever science of the game.

Are there quite a few "three to two" endings that are regular draw positions?

Yes, there are quite a number of ways that two can draw

against three, provided you can get your opponent into these positions.

Perhaps you can show me the ones that occur most often.

Why there are several known as the "Payne" Draws which often come in as life savers at the close of a one-sided game.

Set up the following on your board. Black Kings on 14 and 15, Black single man on 13. White Kings on 22 and 23. In this setting, it is Black's move, yet he cannot win. The moves to the draw are as follows:

Black moves		*White moves*
14-17 . . . . then		.23-26
15-10		.22-18
10-6		.26-30
17-21		.18-22
6-9		.30-26
9-14		.26-30
14-17		.22-18 (a)
17-14 Drawn		

At (a) watch out and don't play 30 to 26, for it gives your opponent a neat win by 21-25, 22-29, 17-22, 26-17, 13-22. Black wins.

Another standard "Payne Draw" is: Black Kings on 18, 19, Black man on 28. White Kings 32, 27, White to move and draw. The Draw moves are 27-24, 18-15, 24-20, 15-11, 20-24, 19-23, 24-20, and Black must concede a draw.

Another Draw with two Kings to three is as follows: Black Kings on 3, 4, and 12. White Kings on 10 and 15. White moves and gets his draw as follows: 15-11, 3-8, 10-15, 8-3, 15-19, 12-8, 19-15. Drawn.

CHAPTER TEN

WHAT ARE THE "TWO"
AND "THREE-MOVE" RESTRICTIONS?

Mr. Hopper, have there been any fundamental changes in the game of checkers during the past century?

The game itself has not had any fundamental change and there is little room for any improvement. However, there have been several new styles of play introduced which have been adopted in some of the bigger tournaments. I refer to what is called the 2-move, and 3-move restrictions style of play.

What are the features of these styles of play?

The "two-move" restriction style originated in England shortly before 1900. Its purpose was to compel the experts to use more variety of play by having them ballot their opening moves.

You mean that Black's first move and White's reply had to be selected by balloting?

Yes, that's it exactly and the way it was done was as follows: At the start of the game, you will note that Black has seven possible moves, 9-13, 9-14, 10-14, 10-15, 11-15, 11-16, and 12-16. These were printed on separate cards and shuffled and the cards cut. Whatever opening move that came up had to be played by Black.

Then White's seven possible replies 24-20, 24-19, 23-19, 23-18, 22-18, 22-17, and 21-17, printed on separate cards were shuffled and cut, and the reply that came up had to be played by White.

For instance, 10-14 may have been cut for Black's first move and 22-17 may have been selected for White's reply. These moves were made on the board and from then on the players played as they chose. Of course, if 9-14, 21-17 came up on the cards another ballot had to be taken for 9-14, 21-17 would lose a checker immediately for White, also 10-14, 21-17 was barred for the same reason.

This must have given quite a combination of opening attacks and defense.

Yes, all told it produced 47 different combinations, not counting the two that were barred.

Mr. Hopper, did not this also produce many openings which gave weak attacks and defense?

Yes it did produce a number of weak openings, four of which being so untenable that they were later included in the barred openings, these were (9-14, 23-18) (10-14, 23-18) (11-16, 23-19) and (12-16, 23-19). When these were balloted, another ballot was taken.

What was the general effect of this system of forcing the players to forgo their usual strong attacks?

Well, it had the general effect of forcing the players to mix things rather than stick to their regular orthodox lines of play. However, it was not long before the leading players began to prepare orthodox lines on all these openings.

As I see it, the purpose of the two-move Restriction was to add more scope to the game. Does that mean that the oldtime way of opening as you please had been exhausted?

By no means. The trouble had been that the foremost players insisted on playing certain favorite openings and played them over and over, the result being that the games ended in draw after draw. In some of the famous matches, many of the games were duplicated move for move to the end of the game.

Yes, but could not one player or the other have varied at different stages of the game and broken up this repetition?

Yes, they certainly could have varied at many stages as there was plenty of scope to the old style of play. However, in all these big matches, the players seemed so afraid of each other's reputation that they were reluctant to go in and mix the fight. Of course, there is always a danger in going off the beaten path, but also there is an opportunity of winning as well.

Did this two-move restriction really accomplish its purpose?

Well, for a while it did, but then the same trouble came up again, the topnotch players finally blazed regular trails for all the two-move openings and once again in the big matches both players seemed satisfied to repeat complete games over and over because they knew that they would result in a Draw. In other words, certain pet lines were adopted and played over move for move.

And what happened then?

Certain members of the checker fraternity decided to go a step further and inaugurate a three-move restriction which compelled a ballot of the first three moves of the game, Black's first move, White's reply and Black's next move.

Mr. Hopper, don't you believe that these restrictions were tending to challenge the primary purpose of the game which meant the privilege of choosing your attacks and defense?

Personally, I felt that they were. More so with the introduction of the three-move restriction, which brought out 138 openings. About one quarter of these were found to be so weak that in many cases a player had to start with what amounted to a losing game.

Mr. Hopper, wouldn't you say that in the first place, before the advent of these two- and three-move restrictions, the fault was with the players in copying each other's moves, rather than in being limited in the scope of their play?

Yes, I'd say that appears to be the answer, for even today, there are still countless thousands of unexplored lines of play in the regular unrestricted game.

If a player wants to mix things, he can do it just as well in the old style. He has several good strong opening moves he can make besides 11-15. Also, if your opponent has the Black and persists in playing 11 to 15 at the start, you can play 22-18, and form the Single Corner. You can play 21-17 and play the Switcher or 23-18, forming the Cross, 24-20 forming the Ayrshire Lassie, 24-19 forming the Second Double Corner or 23-19 forming a whole group of possible openings admitting of an infinite variety of play. I am positive that no two-move or three-move exponent can dare say that he knows anything but a small amount of all the play that can come up in these old standard openings.

However, the student need have no worries when he

knows that 95 per cent of the checkers that is played in the world today is played in the regular good old-fashioned way that has been popular for centuries and will probably continue to be the universal favorite for the vast majority for centuries to come.

....

CHAPTER ELEVEN

FINAL ADVICE TO THE STUDENT

Well, you have given me quite a fascinating insight into the game of checkers. I wonder if you could point out briefly a few more essential points to remember.

Well, I might add a few golden rules, which will not alone help your game but will help promote the good will and friendships of other players.

1. Lose with good grace and sportsmanship and remember that every loss will show you your faults.

2. Look well before you make a move. Never touch a checker until you are sure you are going to move it. By the rules, an opponent can make you move a touched checker. Important matches have been lost by such carelessness.

3. Do not relax and take your mind off the game between moves, for it is easy to lose the train of thought. Experts, when playing opponents of equal caliber, use all the time between moves to advantage in studying the position ahead.

4. Look at every man on the board before you make your move; not only to make certain that all pieces are out of danger, but to plan your strategy a move or two ahead.

5. Do not whistle or drum on the table between the moves as it is unfair to your opponent.

6. Always keep a record of the games you play. In this way, you can review them later and locate where you made a weak or losing move, or if you have won the game, find out where your opponent made his mistake.

7. ORGANIZING A LOCAL CHECKER CLUB. Endeavor to organize a checker club in your town or neighborhood. If you can get a gathering of two or three players and meet regularly, it will add a lot of fun and entertainment. Where there are three players present, you can hold a "get-up" tourney. The loser of each game having to get up and the third player taking his place. This goes on for each game and makes it possible for all three players to participate. There is a lot of fun and excitement to this for each player tries to hold the winning seat.

8. TEAM MATCHES add loads of zest to the game and add to its popularity. If you belong to a club, Y.M.C.A., High School, College or, in fact, any social organization, try and get a half dozen or more players interested in the game. Sometimes there are plenty of checker players around and, if a bulletin is posted announcing a checker club, it will bring in more players than you imagine. After the first few meetings, you can stage a Round Robin tournament and soon locate the best players. You can then pick the six or more best players and form a team. You can challenge other schools or clubs in your locality to a team match.

9. RECREATION CENTERS AND PLAYGROUNDS. Checkers fits in ideally at the Public Playgrounds and Recreation Centers of all the large cities. It is one of the best educational pastimes for the juvenile mind and develops faculties necessary to a successful career—concentration, calculation and adroitness.

10. METROPOLITAN CHECKER LEAGUES. Several principal cities now boast Metropolitan Checker Leagues, composed of teams from the various large banks, utilities and insurance companies and other organizations with a large number of employees. These Leagues' team matches sometimes bring together over a dozen teams, with a total of over a hundred

players in action. The keen rivalry adds lots of pep to these contests.

11. HOW TO START COMPETITION. Where a player lives in some small town and finds it difficult to locate competition, the best suggestion would be to find out what general store, barbershop, or gas station is the village hang-out. There always seems to be some spot in every small town or village where the natives gather to talk over things in general. If you do not see any sign of checkers in these places, just bring in your own board and checkers and you won't have much trouble in finding players to compete with you; in fact, inside of a few weeks, you'll find you have started a hot bed of checkers.

12. CORRESPONDENCE CHECKERS. Where a person is less fortunate and through sickness or infirmity is confined to his home, he can engage in correspondence checkers. This style of play is growing very popular these days, some of the players living hundreds of miles apart. The process is very simple. You can play two or more games at the same time. You start by sending your opponent your first moves with Black in game one. He then writes down his replies against same, also adds his first move with Black in game two. The players exchange postals with their moves until either one or the other loses.

While you have plenty of time to figure out good moves in this style of play, still your opponent has the same advantage and the games grow very very exciting as they near the finish.

When I was just starting to take up checkers, I entered a regular correspondence checker tourney and my name was matched with the town clerk out at Evanston, Wyoming. We played a series of six games which resulted in a tie of two wins each and two drawn. Later, I was matched with a chap in Augusta, Georgia, and besides the fun of playing the games, we built up quite a social friendship, exchanging news of our different localities and swapping interesting yarns about ourselves.

*   *   *

And now, checker friends, before I close my little talks on checker playing, I'd like you all to feel that we have acquired a friendship that will be carried through the years. Perhaps in my travels and exhibition tours, I will have an opportunity of visiting your town or city and have a chance to greet you in person.

Aside from having written a book which I feel will make a lot of crack checker players, I have the inherent satisfaction of knowing I am promoting a game that offers such a blessing to the sick and shut-ins, and likewise affords everyone a mental foundation to build a successful career.

....

CHAPTER TWELVE

"THE STANDARD LAWS OF CHECKERS"

1. The checkerboard must be composed of light and dark squares. The best combination of playing colors being a green and buff board with red and white checkers. In tournament, the standard size board measures 16″ across.

2. The bottom corner of the board, the single corner, must always be on your left and the double corner at your right.

3. The checkers can be any combination of contrasting colors—although red and white is preferable. Other combinations are red and black and black and white. A checker 1¼″ in diameter is the standard size.

4. The Black men are placed on the supposed first 12 squares of the board those numbered 1 to 12, while the Whites occupy the high numbered squares from 21 to 32.

5. Each player alternates with the dark or light checkers, lots being cast for the choice of color for the first game.

6. The Black or dark checkers always make the first move.

7. A player is allowed five minutes to make a move. If it has not been made at that time "time" is called and, at the expiration of another minute he loses the game.

8. In cases where you must jump and there is only one way of jumping, "Time" can be called at the expiration of one minute. If you delay your jump another minute, you forfeit the game.

9. If you wish to arrange your own or your opponent's pieces properly on the squares, you must give intimation of

your intentions to your opponent. If you should adjust pieces on the board without advising your opponent, he can caution you for the first offense and can claim the game for any later offense.

10. After the pieces have been arranged, if the person whose turn it is to play touches one, *he must either play the piece or forfeit the game. When the piece is not playable,* he is cautioned that he will forfeit the game if he commits the same offense again. If any part of the piece is moved in any direction, the piece must be advanced to the next square towards which it was moved.

11. If the hand is withdrawn from the piece after it is played, the play is complete. This also applies in jumping, where several pieces can be jumped at one time. If the hand is withdrawn before all the jumps are completed, the other pieces cannot be taken.

12. Any player who makes a false or improper move loses the game without another move being made.

13. The "huff" or "blow" is the removing of any one of your opponent's pieces that should have jumped. The "huff" or "blow" does not constitute a move.*

14. The player has the power either to "huff" (pick up the piece) or compel the jump.*

15. When any single checker reaches any of the squares on the opposite side of the board, it becomes a King and is "Crowned" by placing a man on top of it. This is done by the opponent and if he neglect to do this, any play shall be put back until your man is crowned. A Crowned King has

* In the laws amended by the American Checker Assn. the "Huff or Blow" is considered obsolete, the players being compelled to make all jumps.

the privilege of moving backwards and forwards as the limits of the play permit.

16. When neither of the players can force a win, the game is adjudged a draw. If one side appears stronger, he is required to complete the win or to show to the satisfaction of the referee a decided advantage within 40 of his own moves.

17. Anything that serves to distract the attention of a player is strictly forbidden. Hovering over the board, making signs or blowing smoke is subject to a warning from the other player and if continued thereafter can cause the player to forfeit the game.

18. Neither player is permitted to leave the room while a game is pending, unless they have sufficient reason and have obtained the other player's consent.

19. Any spectators giving warning by signs or remarks can be ordered from the room during match or tournament play.

20. Tourneys played under the straight "Knock-out" style of play shall consist of as many games as are found necessary to eliminate one of the contestants. In the "Double Knock-out" style, both players are penalized a half-life in the event of a continued tie.

21. Should any dispute occur, not satisfactorily determined by the foregoing laws, the question shall be put up to a disinterested arbiter having a knowledge of the game and his decision shall be final.

In tournaments, the decision of the Tourney Committee shall be final.

MATCH AND TOURNAMENT SCORES

It is interesting to note that the original game of checkers often called *go-as-you please* is still the most popular mode of playing checkers, and likewise has its champions. One of its strongest adherents was Melvin Pomeroy of Binghampton, New York, who not only proved his invincibility at this original style of play, but re-demonstrated its scope by defeating Alfred Jordan in a *go-as-you-please* match contested in 1914. Jordan, who won the *two-move* championship of England, was anxious to annex the *free-style* title. In a return match, in 1915, Pomeroy was again victorious, winning three games and leaving Jordan scoreless. He retained the title until his death in 1933. The more recent matches between Millard Hopper and Tom Wiswell for the *go-as-you-please* championship presented added proof that the original method of playing checkers was far from being exhausted.

WORLD'S THREE-MOVE TITLE

1948 - Walter Hellman (Gary, Indiana) vs. Asa Long (Toledo, Ohio) played at Cedar Point, Ohio. Winner, Hellman. Score 2 to 1 and 47 draws.

1949 - Walter Hellman vs. William F. Ryan (New York City) Score, Hellman 4, Ryan 4 and 42 draws. Hellman retained the title. A return match was scheduled for 1953 but Ryan died in St. Petersburg, Florida a few days before the contest was to be played.

1951 - Walter Hellman vs. Maurice Chamblee. Winner, Hellman. Score, 6 to 1 and 29 draws.

1953 - Walter Hellman vs. Basil Case (Russellville, Ala.) Winner, Hellman. Score, 4 to 1 and 33 draws.

1955 - Walter Hellman vs. Marion Tinsley (Columbus, Ohio) Winner, Tinsley. Score, 3 to 0 and 35 draws. Tinsley becomes *three-move champion.*

1952 - Marion Tinsley (Columbus, Ohio) vs. Newell Banks (Detroit, Michigan) Winner, Tinsley. Score, 3 to 0 and 37 draws. (NOTE: The international status of this title was still undecided until Marion Tinsley traveled to England in 1958 and defeated Derek Oldbury of Bristol, the claimant to the British title.)

GO-AS-YOU-PLEASE WORLD'S TITLE

1951 - Millard Hopper, titlist (Brooklyn, New York) vs. Tom Wiswell, challenger (Brooklyn, New York) Winner, Wiswell. Score 7 to 2 and 27 draws.

1954 - Return match Tom Wiswell vs. Millard Hopper, played at Glasgow, Kentucky. Score, tied 2 to 2 and 42 draws. Wiswell retains the title. (NOTE: The next scheduled match of this style of play will be in the fall of 1956 when the present champion will face the Canadian challenger, Prof. W. R. Fraser of Montreal.)

AMERICAN TOURNAMENTS

1948 - Winner, Marion Tinsley. Runner-up, Maurice Chamblee.

1950 - Winner, Chamblee. Runner-up, Alex Cameron (St. Petersburg, Fla.)

1952 - Winner, Basil Case. Runner-up, Asa Long (Toledo, Ohio.)

1954 - Winner, Tinsley. Runner-up, Basil Case.

ENGLISH CHAMPIONSHIP

1955 - *Three-move title.* Derek Oldbury (Bristol) vs. Samuel Cohen (London). Winner, Oldbury. Score, 4 to 0 and 23 draws.

1955 - *Two-move title.* Winner Derek Oldbury. Runner-up, A. G. Huggins.

BRITISH CHAMPIONSHIP

1955 - *Three-move title.* Derek Oldbury (Bristol) vs. James
Marshall (Fife, Scotland). Winner Oldbury. Score, 8
to 4 and 15 draws. Derek Oldbury thus became the *two-*
and *three-move* English champion as well as the *three-
move* British champion.

The foregoing matches were all officially endorsed by the
American Checker Federation, the governing body of checkers
in the United States, which recognizes the international aspects
of the game and works in harmony with the English and
Scottish Draughts Association. The 1955 officers of the American Checker Federation are: President, B. T. Clifton (Birmingham, Alabama); 1st Vice President, Tom Wiswell (Brooklyn, New York); Secretary, Henry L. Lober (St. Paul, Minnesota); Treasurer, Lee Munger (Indianapolis, Indiana). The
President of the English Draughts Association is Tom West-
lake (Bristol); Secretary, W. H. Russell (Sheffield, England).

Other officially recognized American champions are:
Newell Banks who defeated William Ryan in a contest for
the *Blindfold Championship;* Leonard Hall who holds the
California and *Pacific Coast Title; Northern States Champion*
Milton Loew, winner at the Lakeside, Ohio Tournament
(1955), Runner-up Ed Ebert; and *Southern States Champion
(1955)* Elzy Langdon (Louisville, Kentucky), runner-up
Lloyd Taylor (Birmingham, Alabama). The recognized
American Women's Champion is Gertrude Huntley of Minne-
apolis, Minnesota, who made the best score of any woman
in a National Tournament.

A CATALOG OF SELECTED
DOVER BOOKS
IN ALL FIELDS OF INTEREST

A CATALOG OF SELECTED DOVER

BOOKS IN ALL FIELDS OF INTEREST

CONCERNING THE SPIRITUAL IN ART, Wassily Kandinsky. Pioneering work by father of abstract art. Thoughts on color theory, nature of art. Analysis of earlier masters. 12 illustrations. 80pp. of text. 5⅜ × 8½. 23411-8 Pa. $3.95

ANIMALS: 1,419 Copyright-Free Illustrations of Mammals, Birds, Fish, Insects, etc., Jim Harter (ed.). Clear wood engravings present, in extremely lifelike poses, over 1,000 species of animals. One of the most extensive pictorial sourcebooks of its kind. Captions. Index. 284pp. 9 × 12. 23766-4 Pa. $10.95

CELTIC ART: The Methods of Construction, George Bain. Simple geometric techniques for making Celtic interlacements, spirals, Kells-type initials, animals, humans, etc. Over 500 illustrations. 160pp. 9 × 12. (USO) 22923-8 Pa. $8.95

AN ATLAS OF ANATOMY FOR ARTISTS, Fritz Schider. Most thorough reference work on art anatomy in the world. Hundreds of illustrations, including selections from works by Vesalius, Leonardo, Goya, Ingres, Michelangelo, others. 593 illustrations. 192pp. 7⅛ × 10¼. 20241-0 Pa. $8.95

CELTIC HAND STROKE-BY-STROKE (Irish Half-Uncial from "The Book of Kells"): An Arthur Baker Calligraphy Manual, Arthur Baker. Complete guide to creating each letter of the alphabet in distinctive Celtic manner. Covers hand position, strokes, pens, inks, paper, more. Illustrated. 48pp. 8¼ × 11.
24336-2 Pa. $3.95

EASY ORIGAMI, John Montroll. Charming collection of 32 projects (hat, cup, pelican, piano, swan, many more) specially designed for the novice origami hobbyist. Clearly illustrated easy-to-follow instructions insure that even beginning papercrafters will achieve successful results. 48pp. 8¼ × 11. 27298-2 Pa. $2.95

THE COMPLETE BOOK OF BIRDHOUSE CONSTRUCTION FOR WOOD-WORKERS, Scott D. Campbell. Detailed instructions, illustrations, tables. Also data on bird habitat and instinct patterns. Bibliography. 3 tables. 63 illustrations in 15 figures. 48pp. 5¼ × 8½. 24407-5 Pa. $1.95

BLOOMINGDALE'S ILLUSTRATED 1886 CATALOG: Fashions, Dry Goods and Housewares, Bloomingdale Brothers. Famed merchants' extremely rare catalog depicting about 1,700 products: clothing, housewares, firearms, dry goods, jewelry, more. Invaluable for dating, identifying vintage items. Also, copyright-free graphics for artists, designers. Co-published with Henry Ford Museum & Green-field Village. 160pp. 8¼ × 11. 25780-0 Pa. $8.95

HISTORIC COSTUME IN PICTURES, Braun & Schneider. Over 1,450 costumed figures in clearly detailed engravings—from dawn of civilization to end of 19th century. Captions. Many folk costumes. 256pp. 8⅜ × 11¾. 23150-X Pa. $10.95

STICKLEY CRAFTSMAN FURNITURE CATALOGS, Gustav Stickley and L. & J. G. Stickley. Beautiful, functional furniture in two authentic catalogs from 1910. 594 illustrations, including 277 photos, show settles, rockers, armchairs, reclining chairs, bookcases, desks, tables. 183pp. 6½ × 9¼. 23838-5 Pa. $8.95

AMERICAN LOCOMOTIVES IN HISTORIC PHOTOGRAPHS: 1858 to 1949, Ron Ziel (ed.). A rare collection of 126 meticulously detailed official photographs, called "builder portraits," of American locomotives that majestically chronicle the rise of steam locomotive power in America. Introduction. Detailed captions. xi + 129pp. 9 × 12. 27393-8 Pa. $12.95

AMERICA'S LIGHTHOUSES: An Illustrated History, Francis Ross Holland, Jr. Delightfully written, profusely illustrated fact-filled survey of over 200 American lighthouses since 1716. History, anecdotes, technological advances, more. 240pp. 8 × 10¾. 25576-X Pa. $10.95

TOWARDS A NEW ARCHITECTURE, Le Corbusier. Pioneering manifesto by founder of "International School." Technical and aesthetic theories, views of industry, economics, relation of form to function, "mass-production split" and much more. Profusely illustrated. 320pp. 6⅛ × 9¼. (USO) 25023-7 Pa. $8.95

HOW THE OTHER HALF LIVES, Jacob Riis. Famous journalistic record, exposing poverty and degradation of New York slums around 1900, by major social reformer. 100 striking and influential photographs. 233pp. 10 × 7⅞.
22012-5 Pa $10.95

FRUIT KEY AND TWIG KEY TO TREES AND SHRUBS, William M. Harlow. One of the handiest and most widely used identification aids. Fruit key covers 120 deciduous and evergreen species; twig key 160 deciduous species. Easily used. Over 300 photographs. 126pp. 5⅜ × 8½. 20511-8 Pa. $2.95

COMMON BIRD SONGS, Dr. Donald J. Borror. Songs of 60 most common U.S. birds: robins, sparrows, cardinals, bluejays, finches, more—arranged in order of increasing complexity. Up to 9 variations of songs of each species.
Cassette and manual 99911-4 $8.95

ORCHIDS AS HOUSE PLANTS, Rebecca Tyson Northen. Grow cattleyas and many other kinds of orchids—in a window, in a case, or under artificial light. 63 illustrations. 148pp. 5⅜ × 8½. 23261-1 Pa. $3.95

MONSTER MAZES, Dave Phillips. Masterful mazes at four levels of difficulty. Avoid deadly perils and evil creatures to find magical treasures. Solutions for all 32 exciting illustrated puzzles. 48pp. 8¼ × 11. 26005-4 Pa. $2.95

MOZART'S DON GIOVANNI (DOVER OPERA LIBRETTO SERIES), Wolfgang Amadeus Mozart. Introduced and translated by Ellen H. Bleiler. Standard Italian libretto, with complete English translation. Convenient and thoroughly portable—an ideal companion for reading along with a recording or the performance itself. Introduction. List of characters. Plot summary. 121pp. 5¼ × 8½.
24944-1 Pa. $2.95

TECHNICAL MANUAL AND DICTIONARY OF CLASSICAL BALLET, Gail Grant. Defines, explains, comments on steps, movements, poses and concepts. 15-page pictorial section. Basic book for student, viewer. 127pp. 5⅜ × 8½.
21843-0 Pa. $3.95

BRASS INSTRUMENTS: Their History and Development, Anthony Baines. Authoritative, updated survey of the evolution of trumpets, trombones, bugles, cornets, French horns, tubas and other brass wind instruments. Over 140 illustrations and 48 music examples. Corrected and updated by author. New preface. Bibliography. 320pp. 5⅜ × 8½. 27574-4 Pa. $9.95

HOLLYWOOD GLAMOR PORTRAITS, John Kobal (ed.). 145 photos from 1926–49. Harlow, Gable, Bogart, Bacall; 94 stars in all. Full background on photographers, technical aspects. 160pp. 8⅜ × 11¼. 23352-9 Pa. $9.95

MAX AND MORITZ, Wilhelm Busch. Great humor classic in both German and English. Also 10 other works: "Cat and Mouse," "Plisch and Plumm," etc. 216pp. 5⅜ × 8½. 20181-3 Pa. $5.95

THE RAVEN AND OTHER FAVORITE POEMS, Edgar Allan Poe. Over 40 of the author's most memorable poems: "The Bells," "Ulalume," "Israfel," "To Helen," "The Conqueror Worm," "Eldorado," "Annabel Lee," many more. Alphabetic lists of titles and first lines. 64pp. 5³⁄₁₆ × 8¼. 26685-0 Pa. $1.00

SEVEN SCIENCE FICTION NOVELS, H. G. Wells. The standard collection of the great novels. Complete, unabridged. First Men in the Moon, Island of Dr. Moreau, War of the Worlds, Food of the Gods, Invisible Man, Time Machine, In the Days of the Comet. Total of 1,015pp. 5⅜ × 8½. (USO) 20264-X Clothbd. $29.95

AMULETS AND SUPERSTITIONS, E. A. Wallis Budge. Comprehensive discourse on origin, powers of amulets in many ancient cultures: Arab, Persian, Babylonian, Assyrian, Egyptian, Gnostic, Hebrew, Phoenician, Syriac, etc. Covers cross, swastika, crucifix, seals, rings, stones, etc. 584pp. 5⅜ × 8½. 23573-4 Pa. $10.95

RUSSIAN STORIES/PYCCKHE PACCKA3bl: A Dual-Language Book, edited by Gleb Struve. Twelve tales by such masters as Chekhov, Tolstoy, Dostoevsky, Pushkin, others. Excellent word-for-word English translations on facing pages, plus teaching and study aids, Russian/English vocabulary, biographical/critical introductions, more. 416pp. 5⅜ × 8½. 26244-8 Pa. $7.95

PHILADELPHIA THEN AND NOW: 60 Sites Photographed in the Past and Present, Kenneth Finkel and Susan Oyama. Rare photographs of City Hall, Logan Square, Independence Hall, Betsy Ross House, other landmarks juxtaposed with contemporary views. Captures changing face of historic city. Introduction. Captions. 128pp. 8¼ × 11. 25790-8 Pa. $9.95

AIA ARCHITECTURAL GUIDE TO NASSAU AND SUFFOLK COUNTIES, LONG ISLAND, The American Institute of Architects, Long Island Chapter, and the Society for the Preservation of Long Island Antiquities. Comprehensive, well-researched and generously illustrated volume brings to life over three centuries of Long Island's great architectural heritage. More than 240 photographs with authoritative, extensively detailed captions. 176pp. 8¼ × 11. 26946-9 Pa. $14.95

NORTH AMERICAN INDIAN LIFE: Customs and Traditions of 23 Tribes, Elsie Clews Parsons (ed.). 27 fictionalized essays by noted anthropologists examine religion, customs, government, additional facets of life among the Winnebago, Crow, Zuni, Eskimo, other tribes. 480pp. 6⅛ × 9¼. 27377-6 Pa. $10.95

FRANK LLOYD WRIGHT'S HOLLYHOCK HOUSE, Donald Hoffmann. Lavishly illustrated, carefully documented study of one of Wright's most controversial residential designs. Over 120 photographs, floor plans, elevations, etc. Detailed perceptive text by noted Wright scholar. Index. 128pp. 9¼ × 10¾.
27133-1 Pa. $10.95

THE MALE AND FEMALE FIGURE IN MOTION: 60 Classic Photographic Sequences, Eadweard Muybridge. 60 true-action photographs of men and women walking, running, climbing, bending, turning, etc., reproduced from rare 19th-century masterpiece. vi + 121pp. 9 × 12. 24745-7 Pa. $10.95

1001 QUESTIONS ANSWERED ABOUT THE SEASHORE, N. J. Berrill and Jacquelyn Berrill. Queries answered about dolphins, sea snails, sponges, starfish, fishes, shore birds, many others. Covers appearance, breeding, growth, feeding, much more. 305pp. 5¼ × 8¼. 23366-9 Pa. $7.95

GUIDE TO OWL WATCHING IN NORTH AMERICA, Donald S. Heintzelman. Superb guide offers complete data and descriptions of 19 species: barn owl, screech owl, snowy owl, many more. Expert coverage of owl-watching equipment, conservation, migrations and invasions, etc. Guide to observing sites. 84 illustrations. xiii + 193pp. 5⅜ × 8½. 27344-X Pa. $7.95

MEDICINAL AND OTHER USES OF NORTH AMERICAN PLANTS: A Historical Survey with Special Reference to the Eastern Indian Tribes, Charlotte Erichsen-Brown. Chronological historical citations document 500 years of usage of plants, trees, shrubs native to eastern Canada, northeastern U.S. Also complete identifying information. 343 illustrations. 544pp. 6½ × 9¼. 25951-X Pa. $12.95

STORYBOOK MAZES, Dave Phillips. 23 stories and mazes on two-page spreads: Wizard of Oz, Treasure Island, Robin Hood, etc. Solutions. 64pp. 8¼ × 11.
23628-5 Pa. $2.95

NEGRO FOLK MUSIC, U.S.A., Harold Courlander. Noted folklorist's scholarly yet readable analysis of rich and varied musical tradition. Includes authentic versions of over 40 folk songs. Valuable bibliography and discography. xi + 324pp. 5⅜ × 8½. 27350-4 Pa. $7.95

MOVIE-STAR PORTRAITS OF THE FORTIES, John Kobal (ed.). 163 glamor, studio photos of 106 stars of the 1940s: Rita Hayworth, Ava Gardner, Marlon Brando, Clark Gable, many more. 176pp. 8⅜ × 11¼. 23546-7 Pa. $10.95

BENCHLEY LOST AND FOUND, Robert Benchley. Finest humor from early 30s, about pet peeves, child psychologists, post office and others. Mostly unavailable elsewhere. 73 illustrations by Peter Arno and others. 183pp. 5⅜ × 8½.
22410-4 Pa. $4.95

YEKL and THE IMPORTED BRIDEGROOM AND OTHER STORIES OF YIDDISH NEW YORK, Abraham Cahan. Film Hester Street based on Yekl (1896). Novel, other stories among first about Jewish immigrants on N.Y.'s East Side. 240pp. 5⅜ × 8½. 22427-9 Pa. $5.95

SELECTED POEMS, Walt Whitman. Generous sampling from *Leaves of Grass*. Twenty-four poems include "I Hear America Singing," "Song of the Open Road," "I Sing the Body Electric," "When Lilacs Last in the Dooryard Bloom'd," "O Captain! My Captain!"—all reprinted from an authoritative edition. Lists of titles and first lines. 128pp. 5³⁄₁₆ × 8¼. 26878-0 Pa. $1.00

THE BEST TALES OF HOFFMANN, E. T. A. Hoffmann. 10 of Hoffmann's most important stories: "Nutcracker and the King of Mice," "The Golden Flowerpot," etc. 458pp. 5⅜ × 8½. 21793-0 Pa. $8.95

FROM FETISH TO GOD IN ANCIENT EGYPT, E. A. Wallis Budge. Rich detailed survey of Egyptian conception of "God" and gods, magic, cult of animals, Osiris, more. Also, superb English translations of hymns and legends. 240 illustrations. 545pp. 5⅜ × 8½. 25803-3 Pa. $10.95

FRENCH STORIES/CONTES FRANÇAIS: A Dual-Language Book, Wallace Fowlie. Ten stories by French masters, Voltaire to Camus: "Micromegas" by Voltaire; "The Atheist's Mass" by Balzac; "Minuet" by de Maupassant; "The Guest" by Camus, six more. Excellent English translations on facing pages. Also French-English vocabulary list, exercises, more. 352pp. 5⅜ × 8½. 26443-2 Pa. $8.95

CHICAGO AT THE TURN OF THE CENTURY IN PHOTOGRAPHS: 122 Historic Views from the Collections of the Chicago Historical Society, Larry A. Viskochil. Rare large-format prints offer detailed views of City Hall, State Street, the Loop, Hull House, Union Station, many other landmarks, circa 1904–1913. Introduction. Captions. Maps. 144pp. 9⅜ × 12¼. 24656-6 Pa. $12.95

OLD BROOKLYN IN EARLY PHOTOGRAPHS, 1865–1929, William Lee Younger. Luna Park, Gravesend race track, construction of Grand Army Plaza, moving of Hotel Brighton, etc. 157 previously unpublished photographs. 165pp. 8⅞ × 11¾. 23587-4 Pa. $12.95

THE MYTHS OF THE NORTH AMERICAN INDIANS, Lewis Spence. Rich anthology of the myths and legends of the Algonquins, Iroquois, Pawnees and Sioux, prefaced by an extensive historical and ethnological commentary. 36 illustrations. 480pp. 5⅜ × 8½. 25967-6 Pa. $8.95

AN ENCYCLOPEDIA OF BATTLES: Accounts of Over 1,560 Battles from 1479 B.C. to the Present, David Eggenberger. Essential details of every major battle in recorded history from the first battle of Megiddo in 1479 B.C. to Grenada in 1984. List of Battle Maps. New Appendix covering the years 1967–1984. Index. 99 illustrations. 544pp. 6½ × 9¼. 24913-1 Pa. $14.95

SAILING ALONE AROUND THE WORLD, Captain Joshua Slocum. First man to sail around the world, alone, in small boat. One of great feats of seamanship told in delightful manner. 67 illustrations. 294pp. 5⅜ × 8½. 20326-3 Pa. $4.95

ANARCHISM AND OTHER ESSAYS, Emma Goldman. Powerful, penetrating, prophetic essays on direct action, role of minorities, prison reform, puritan hypocrisy, violence, etc. 271pp. 5⅜ × 8½. 22484-8 Pa. $5.95

MYTHS OF THE HINDUS AND BUDDHISTS, Ananda K. Coomaraswamy and Sister Nivedita. Great stories of the epics; deeds of Krishna, Shiva, taken from puranas, Vedas, folk tales; etc. 32 illustrations. 400pp. 5⅜ × 8½. 21759-0 Pa. $8.95

BEYOND PSYCHOLOGY, Otto Rank. Fear of death, desire of immortality, nature of sexuality, social organization, creativity, according to Rankian system. 291pp. 5⅜ × 8½. 20485-5 Pa. $7.95

A THEOLOGICO-POLITICAL TREATISE, Benedict Spinoza. Also contains unfinished Political Treatise. Great classic on religious liberty, theory of government on common consent. R. Elwes translation. Total of 421pp. 5⅜ × 8½. 20249-6 Pa. $7.95

MY BONDAGE AND MY FREEDOM, Frederick Douglass. Born a slave, Douglass became outspoken force in antislavery movement. The best of Douglass' autobiographies. Graphic description of slave life. 464pp. 5⅜ × 8½.   22457-0 Pa. $7.95

FOLLOWING THE EQUATOR: A Journey Around the World, Mark Twain. Fascinating humorous account of 1897 voyage to Hawaii, Australia, India, New Zealand, etc. Ironic, bemused reports on peoples, customs, climate, flora and fauna, politics, much more. 197 illustrations. 720pp. 5⅜ × 8½.   26113-1 Pa. $15.95

THE PEOPLE CALLED SHAKERS, Edward D. Andrews. Definitive study of Shakers: origins, beliefs, practices, dances, social organization, furniture and crafts, etc. 33 illustrations. 351pp. 5⅜ × 8½.   21081-2 Pa. $7.95

THE MYTHS OF GREECE AND ROME, H. A. Guerber. A classic of mythology, generously illustrated, long prized for its simple, graphic, accurate retelling of the principal myths of Greece and Rome, and for its commentary on their origins and significance. With 64 illustrations by Michelangelo, Raphael, Titian, Rubens, Canova, Bernini and others. 480pp. 5⅜ × 8½.   27584-1 Pa. $9.95

PSYCHOLOGY OF MUSIC, Carl E. Seashore. Classic work discusses music as a medium from psychological viewpoint. Clear treatment of physical acoustics, auditory apparatus, sound perception, development of musical skills, nature of musical feeling, host of other topics. 88 figures. 408pp. 5⅜ × 8½.   21851-1 Pa. $8.95

THE PHILOSOPHY OF HISTORY, Georg W. Hegel. Great classic of Western thought develops concept that history is not chance but rational process, the evolution of freedom. 457pp. 5⅜ × 8½.   20112-0 Pa. $8.95

THE BOOK OF TEA, Kakuzo Okakura. Minor classic of the Orient: entertaining, charming explanation, interpretation of traditional Japanese culture in terms of tea ceremony. 94pp. 5⅜ × 8½.   20070-1 Pa. $2.95

LIFE IN ANCIENT EGYPT, Adolf Erman. Fullest, most thorough, detailed older account with much not in more recent books, domestic life, religion, magic, medicine, commerce, much more. Many illustrations reproduce tomb paintings, carvings, hieroglyphs, etc. 597pp. 5⅜ × 8½.   22632-8 Pa. $9.95

SUNDIALS, Their Theory and Construction, Albert Waugh. Far and away the best, most thorough coverage of ideas, mathematics concerned, types, construction, adjusting anywhere. Simple, nontechnical treatment allows even children to build several of these dials. Over 100 illustrations. 230pp. 5⅜ × 8½.   22947-5 Pa. $5.95

DYNAMICS OF FLUIDS IN POROUS MEDIA, Jacob Bear. For advanced students of ground water hydrology, soil mechanics and physics, drainage and irrigation engineering, and more. 335 illustrations. Exercises, with answers. 784pp. 6⅛ × 9¼.   65675-6 Pa. $19.95

SONGS OF EXPERIENCE: Facsimile Reproduction with 26 Plates in Full Color, William Blake. 26 full-color plates from a rare 1826 edition. Includes "The Tyger," "London," "Holy Thursday," and other poems. Printed text of poems. 48pp. 5¼ × 7.   24636-1 Pa. $3.95

OLD-TIME VIGNETTES IN FULL COLOR, Carol Belanger Grafton (ed.). Over 390 charming, often sentimental illustrations, selected from archives of Victorian graphics—pretty women posing, children playing, food, flowers, kittens and puppies, smiling cherubs, birds and butterflies, much more. All copyright-free. 48pp. 9¼ × 12¼.   27269-9 Pa. $5.95

PERSPECTIVE FOR ARTISTS, Rex Vicat Cole. Depth, perspective of sky and sea, shadows, much more, not usually covered. 391 diagrams, 81 reproductions of drawings and paintings. 279pp. 5⅜ × 8½. 22487-2 Pa. $6.95

DRAWING THE LIVING FIGURE, Joseph Sheppard. Innovative approach to artistic anatomy focuses on specifics of surface anatomy, rather than muscles and bones. Over 170 drawings of live models in front, back and side views, and in widely varying poses. Accompanying diagrams. 177 illustrations. Introduction. Index. 144pp. 8⅜ × 11¼. 26723-7 Pa. $7.95

GOTHIC AND OLD ENGLISH ALPHABETS: 100 Complete Fonts, Dan X. Solo. Add power, elegance to posters, signs, other graphics with 100 stunning copyright-free alphabets: Blackstone, Dolbey, Germania, 97 more—including many lower-case, numerals, punctuation marks. 104pp. 8⅛ × 11. 24695-7 Pa. $6.95

HOW TO DO BEADWORK, Mary White. Fundamental book on craft from simple projects to five-bead chains and woven works. 106 illustrations. 142pp. 5⅜ × 8. 20697-1 Pa. $4.95

THE BOOK OF WOOD CARVING, Charles Marshall Sayers. Finest book for beginners discusses fundamentals and offers 34 designs. "Absolutely first rate . . . well thought out and well executed."—E. J. Tangerman. 118pp. 7¾ × 10⅝. 23654-4 Pa. $5.95

ILLUSTRATED CATALOG OF CIVIL WAR MILITARY GOODS: Union Army Weapons, Insignia, Uniform Accessories, and Other Equipment, Schuyler, Hartley, and Graham. Rare, profusely illustrated 1846 catalog includes Union Army uniform and dress regulations, arms and ammunition, coats, insignia, flags, swords, rifles, etc. 226 illustrations. 160pp. 9 × 12. 24939-5 Pa. $10.95

WOMEN'S FASHIONS OF THE EARLY 1900s: An Unabridged Republication of "New York Fashions, 1909," National Cloak & Suit Co. Rare catalog of mail-order fashions documents women's and children's clothing styles shortly after the turn of the century. Captions offer full descriptions, prices. Invaluable resource for fashion, costume historians. Approximately 725 illustrations. 128pp. 8⅜ × 11¼. 27276-1 Pa. $10.95

THE 1912 AND 1915 GUSTAV STICKLEY FURNITURE CATALOGS, Gustav Stickley. With over 200 detailed illustrations and descriptions, these two catalogs are essential reading and reference materials and identification guides for Stickley furniture. Captions cite materials, dimensions and prices. 112pp. 6½ × 9¼. 26676-1 Pa. $9.95

EARLY AMERICAN LOCOMOTIVES, John H. White, Jr. Finest locomotive engravings from early 19th century: historical (1804–74), main-line (after 1870), special, foreign, etc. 147 plates. 142pp. 11⅜ × 8¼. 22772-3 Pa. $8.95

THE TALL SHIPS OF TODAY IN PHOTOGRAPHS, Frank O. Braynard. Lavishly illustrated tribute to nearly 100 majestic contemporary sailing vessels: Amerigo Vespucci, Clearwater, Constitution, Eagle, Mayflower, Sea Cloud, Victory, many more. Authoritative captions provide statistics, background on each ship. 190 black-and-white photographs and illustrations. Introduction. 128pp. 8⅞ × 11¾. 27163-3 Pa. $12.95

EARLY NINETEENTH-CENTURY CRAFTS AND TRADES, Peter Stockham (ed.). Extremely rare 1807 volume describes to youngsters the crafts and trades of the day: brickmaker, weaver, dressmaker, bookbinder, ropemaker, saddler, many more. Quaint prose, charming illustrations for each craft. 20 black-and-white line illustrations. 192pp. $4\frac{5}{8} \times 6$. 27293-1 Pa. $4.95

VICTORIAN FASHIONS AND COSTUMES FROM HARPER'S BAZAR, 1867–1898, Stella Blum (ed.). Day costumes, evening wear, sports clothes, shoes, hats, other accessories in over 1,000 detailed engravings. 320pp. $9\frac{3}{8} \times 12\frac{1}{4}$. 22990-4 Pa. $12.95

GUSTAV STICKLEY, THE CRAFTSMAN, Mary Ann Smith. Superb study surveys broad scope of Stickley's achievement, especially in architecture. Design philosophy, rise and fall of the Craftsman empire, descriptions and floor plans for many Craftsman houses, more. 86 black-and-white halftones. 31 line illustrations. Introduction. 208pp. $6\frac{1}{2} \times 9\frac{1}{4}$. 27210-9 Pa. $9.95

THE LONG ISLAND RAIL ROAD IN EARLY PHOTOGRAPHS, Ron Ziel. Over 220 rare photos, informative text document origin (1844) and development of rail service on Long Island. Vintage views of early trains, locomotives, stations, passengers, crews, much more. Captions. $8\frac{7}{8} \times 11\frac{3}{4}$. 26301-0 Pa. $13.95

THE BOOK OF OLD SHIPS: From Egyptian Galleys to Clipper Ships, Henry B. Culver. Superb, authoritative history of sailing vessels, with 80 magnificent line illustrations. Galley, bark, caravel, longship, whaler, many more. Detailed, informative text on each vessel by noted naval historian. Introduction. 256pp. $5\frac{3}{8} \times 8\frac{1}{2}$. 27332-6 Pa. $6.95

TEN BOOKS ON ARCHITECTURE, Vitruvius. The most important book ever written on architecture. Early Roman aesthetics, technology, classical orders, site selection, all other aspects. Morgan translation. 331pp. $5\frac{3}{8} \times 8\frac{1}{2}$. 20645-9 Pa. $8.95

THE HUMAN FIGURE IN MOTION, Eadweard Muybridge. More than 4,500 stopped-action photos, in action series, showing undraped men, women, children jumping, lying down, throwing, sitting, wrestling, carrying, etc. 390pp. $7\frac{7}{8} \times 10\frac{5}{8}$. 20204-6 Clothbd. $24.95

TREES OF THE EASTERN AND CENTRAL UNITED STATES AND CANADA, William M. Harlow. Best one-volume guide to 140 trees. Full descriptions, woodlore, range, etc. Over 600 illustrations. Handy size. 288pp. $4\frac{1}{2} \times 6\frac{3}{8}$. 20395-6 Pa. $4.95

SONGS OF WESTERN BIRDS, Dr. Donald J. Borror. Complete song and call repertoire of 60 western species, including flycatchers, juncoes, cactus wrens, many more—includes fully illustrated booklet. Cassette and manual 99913-0 $8.95

GROWING AND USING HERBS AND SPICES, Milo Miloradovich. Versatile handbook provides all the information needed for cultivation and use of all the herbs and spices available in North America. 4 illustrations. Index. Glossary. 236pp. $5\frac{3}{8} \times 8\frac{1}{2}$. 25058-X Pa. $5.95

BIG BOOK OF MAZES AND LABYRINTHS, Walter Shepherd. 50 mazes and labyrinths in all—classical, solid, ripple, and more—in one great volume. Perfect inexpensive puzzler for clever youngsters. Full solutions. 112pp. $8\frac{1}{8} \times 11$. 22951-3 Pa. $3.95

PIANO TUNING, J. Cree Fischer. Clearest, best book for beginner, amateur. Simple repairs, raising dropped notes, tuning by easy method of flattened fifths. No previous skills needed. 4 illustrations. 201pp. 5⅜ × 8½. 23267-0 Pa. $4.95

A SOURCE BOOK IN THEATRICAL HISTORY, A. M. Nagler. Contemporary observers on acting, directing, make-up, costuming, stage props, machinery, scene design, from Ancient Greece to Chekhov. 611pp. 5⅜ × 8½. 20515-0 Pa. $10.95

THE COMPLETE NONSENSE OF EDWARD LEAR, Edward Lear. All nonsense limericks, zany alphabets, Owl and Pussycat, songs, nonsense botany, etc., illustrated by Lear. Total of 320pp. 5⅜ × 8½. (USO) 20167-8 Pa. $5.95

VICTORIAN PARLOUR POETRY: An Annotated Anthology, Michael R. Turner. 117 gems by Longfellow, Tennyson, Browning, many lesser-known poets. "The Village Blacksmith," "Curfew Must Not Ring Tonight," "Only a Baby Small," dozens more, often difficult to find elsewhere. Index of poets, titles, first lines. xxiii + 325pp. 5⅜ × 8¼. 27044-0 Pa. $7.95

DUBLINERS, James Joyce. Fifteen stories offer vivid, tightly focused observations of the lives of Dublin's poorer classes. At least one, "The Dead," is considered a masterpiece. Reprinted complete and unabridged from standard edition. 160pp. 5³/₁₆ × 8¼. 26870-5 Pa. $1.00

THE HAUNTED MONASTERY and THE CHINESE MAZE MURDERS, Robert van Gulik. Two full novels by van Gulik, set in 7th-century China, continue adventures of Judge Dee and his companions. An evil Taoist monastery, seemingly supernatural events; overgrown topiary maze hides strange crimes. 27 illustrations. 328pp. 5⅜ × 8½. 23502-5 Pa. $7.95

THE BOOK OF THE SACRED MAGIC OF ABRAMELIN THE MAGE, translated by S. MacGregor Mathers. Medieval manuscript of ceremonial magic. Basic document in Aleister Crowley, Golden Dawn groups. 268pp. 5⅜ × 8½. 23211-5 Pa. $7.95

NEW RUSSIAN-ENGLISH AND ENGLISH-RUSSIAN DICTIONARY, M. A. O'Brien. This is a remarkably handy Russian dictionary, containing a surprising amount of information, including over 70,000 entries. 366pp. 4½ × 6⅛. 20208-9 Pa. $8.95

HISTORIC HOMES OF THE AMERICAN PRESIDENTS, Second, Revised Edition, Irvin Haas. A traveler's guide to American Presidential homes, most open to the public, depicting and describing homes occupied by every American President from George Washington to George Bush. With visiting hours, admission charges, travel routes. 175 photographs. Index. 160pp. 8¼ × 11. 26751-2 Pa. $10.95

NEW YORK IN THE FORTIES, Andreas Feininger. 162 brilliant photographs by the well-known photographer, formerly with *Life* magazine. Commuters, shoppers, Times Square at night, much else from city at its peak. Captions by John von Hartz. 181pp. 9¼ × 10¾. 23585-8 Pa. $12.95

INDIAN SIGN LANGUAGE, William Tomkins. Over 525 signs developed by Sioux and other tribes. Written instructions and diagrams. Also 290 pictographs. 111pp. 6⅛ × 9¼. 22029-X Pa. $3.50

ANATOMY: A Complete Guide for Artists, Joseph Sheppard. A master of figure drawing shows artists how to render human anatomy convincingly. Over 460 illustrations. 224pp. 8⅜ × 11¼. 27279-6 Pa. $9.95

MEDIEVAL CALLIGRAPHY: Its History and Technique, Marc Drogin. Spirited history, comprehensive instruction manual covers 13 styles (ca. 4th century thru 15th). Excellent photographs; directions for duplicating medieval techniques with modern tools. 224pp. 8⅜ × 11¼. 26142-5 Pa. $11.95

DRIED FLOWERS: How to Prepare Them, Sarah Whitlock and Martha Rankin. Complete instructions on how to use silica gel, meal and borax, perlite aggregate, sand and borax, glycerine and water to create attractive permanent flower arrangements. 12 illustrations. 32pp. 5⅜ × 8½. 21802-3 Pa. $1.00

EASY-TO-MAKE BIRD FEEDERS FOR WOODWORKERS, Scott D. Campbell. Detailed, simple-to-use guide for designing, constructing, caring for and using feeders. Text, illustrations for 12 classic and contemporary designs. 96pp. 5⅜ × 8½. 25847-5 Pa. $2.95

OLD-TIME CRAFTS AND TRADES, Peter Stockham. An 1807 book created to teach children about crafts and trades open to them as future careers. It describes in detailed, nontechnical terms 24 different occupations, among them coachmaker, gardener, hairdresser, lacemaker, shoemaker, wheelwright, copper-plate printer, milliner, trunkmaker, merchant and brewer. Finely detailed engravings illustrate each occupation. 192pp. 4⅝ × 6. 27398-9 Pa. $4.95

THE HISTORY OF UNDERCLOTHES, C. Willett Cunnington and Phyllis Cunnington. Fascinating, well-documented survey covering six centuries of English undergarments, enhanced with over 100 illustrations: 12th-century laced-up bodice, footed long drawers (1795), 19th-century bustles, 19th-century corsets for men, Victorian "bust improvers," much more. 272pp. 5⅜ × 8¼. 27124-2 Pa. $9.95

ARTS AND CRAFTS FURNITURE: The Complete Brooks Catalog of 1912, Brooks Manufacturing Co. Photos and detailed descriptions of more than 150 now very collectible furniture designs from the Arts and Crafts movement depict davenports, settees, buffets, desks, tables, chairs, bedsteads, dressers and more, all built of solid, quarter-sawed oak. Invaluable for students and enthusiasts of antiques, Americana and the decorative arts. 80pp. 6½ × 9¼. 27471-3 Pa. $7.95

HOW WE INVENTED THE AIRPLANE: An Illustrated History, Orville Wright. Fascinating firsthand account covers early experiments, construction of planes and motors, first flights, much more. Introduction and commentary by Fred C. Kelly. 76 photographs. 96pp. 8¼ × 11. 25662-6 Pa. $7.95

THE ARTS OF THE SAILOR: Knotting, Splicing and Ropework, Hervey Garrett Smith. Indispensable shipboard reference covers tools, basic knots and useful hitches; handsewing and canvas work, more. Over 100 illustrations. Delightful reading for sea lovers. 256pp. 5⅜ × 8½. 26440-8 Pa. $6.95

FRANK LLOYD WRIGHT'S FALLINGWATER: The House and Its History, Second, Revised Edition, Donald Hoffmann. A total revision—both in text and illustrations—of the standard document on Fallingwater, the boldest, most personal architectural statement of Wright's mature years, updated with valuable new material from the recently opened Frank Lloyd Wright Archives. "Fascinating"—*The New York Times*. 116 illustrations. 128pp. 9¼ × 10¾. 27430-6 Pa. $10.95

PHOTOGRAPHIC SKETCHBOOK OF THE CIVIL WAR, Alexander Gardner. 100 photos taken on field during the Civil War. Famous shots of Manassas, Harper's Ferry, Lincoln, Richmond, slave pens, etc. 244pp. 10⅝ × 8¼.
22731-6 Pa. $9.95

FIVE ACRES AND INDEPENDENCE, Maurice G. Kains. Great back-to-the-land classic explains basics of self-sufficient farming. The one book to get. 95 illustrations. 397pp. 5⅜ × 8½.
20974-1 Pa. $6.95

SONGS OF EASTERN BIRDS, Dr. Donald J. Borror. Songs and calls of 60 species most common to eastern U.S.: warblers, woodpeckers, flycatchers, thrushes, larks, many more in high-quality recording.
Cassette and manual 99912-2 $8.95

A MODERN HERBAL, Margaret Grieve. Much the fullest, most exact, most useful compilation of herbal material. Gigantic alphabetical encyclopedia, from aconite to zedoary, gives botanical information, medical properties, folklore, economic uses, much else. Indispensable to serious reader. 161 illustrations. 888pp. 6½ × 9¼. 2-vol. set. (USO)
Vol. I: 22798-7 Pa. $9.95
Vol. II: 22799-5 Pa. $9.95

HIDDEN TREASURE MAZE BOOK, Dave Phillips. Solve 34 challenging mazes accompanied by heroic tales of adventure. Evil dragons, people-eating plants, bloodthirsty giants, many more dangerous adversaries lurk at every twist and turn. 34 mazes, stories, solutions. 48pp. 8¼ × 11.
24566-7 Pa. $2.95

LETTERS OF W. A. MOZART, Wolfgang A. Mozart. Remarkable letters show bawdy wit, humor, imagination, musical insights, contemporary musical world; includes some letters from Leopold Mozart. 276pp. 5⅜ × 8½.
22859-2 Pa. $6.95

BASIC PRINCIPLES OF CLASSICAL BALLET, Agrippina Vaganova. Great Russian theoretician, teacher explains methods for teaching classical ballet. 118 illustrations. 175pp. 5⅜ × 8½.
22036-2 Pa. $3.95

THE JUMPING FROG, Mark Twain. Revenge edition. The original story of The Celebrated Jumping Frog of Calaveras County, a hapless French translation, and Twain's hilarious "retranslation" from the French. 12 illustrations. 66pp. 5⅜ × 8½.
22686-7 Pa. $3.50

BEST REMEMBERED POEMS, Martin Gardner (ed.). The 126 poems in this superb collection of 19th- and 20th-century British and American verse range from Shelley's "To a Skylark" to the impassioned "Renascence" of Edna St. Vincent Millay and to Edward Lear's whimsical "The Owl and the Pussycat." 224pp. 5⅜ × 8½.
27165-X Pa. $3.95

COMPLETE SONNETS, William Shakespeare. Over 150 exquisite poems deal with love, friendship, the tyranny of time, beauty's evanescence, death and other themes in language of remarkable power, precision and beauty. Glossary of archaic terms. 80pp. 5³⁄₁₆ × 8¼.
26686-9 Pa. $1.00

BODIES IN A BOOKSHOP, R. T. Campbell. Challenging mystery of blackmail and murder with ingenious plot and superbly drawn characters. In the best tradition of British suspense fiction. 192pp. 5⅜ × 8½.
24720-1 Pa. $5.95

THE WIT AND HUMOR OF OSCAR WILDE, Alvin Redman (ed.). More than 1,000 ripostes, paradoxes, wisecracks: Work is the curse of the drinking classes; I can resist everything except temptation; etc. 258pp. 5⅜ × 8½.   20602-5 Pa. $4.95

SHAKESPEARE LEXICON AND QUOTATION DICTIONARY, Alexander Schmidt. Full definitions, locations, shades of meaning in every word in plays and poems. More than 50,000 exact quotations. 1,485pp. 6½ × 9¼. 2-vol. set.
Vol. 1: 22726-X Pa. $15.95
Vol. 2: 22727-8 Pa. $15.95

SELECTED POEMS, Emily Dickinson. Over 100 best-known, best-loved poems by one of America's foremost poets, reprinted from authoritative early editions. No comparable edition at this price. Index of first lines. 64pp. 5³/₁₆ × 8¼.
26466-1 Pa. $1.00

CELEBRATED CASES OF JUDGE DEE (DEE GOONG AN), translated by Robert van Gulik. Authentic 18th-century Chinese detective novel; Dee and associates solve three interlocked cases. Led to van Gulik's own stories with same characters. Extensive introduction. 9 illustrations. 237pp. 5⅜ × 8½.
23337-5 Pa. $5.95

THE MALLEUS MALEFICARUM OF KRAMER AND SPRENGER, translated by Montague Summers. Full text of most important witchhunter's "bible," used by both Catholics and Protestants. 278pp. 6⅝ × 10.   22802-9 Pa. $10.95

SPANISH STORIES/CUENTOS ESPAÑOLES: A Dual-Language Book, Angel Flores (ed.). Unique format offers 13 great stories in Spanish by Cervantes, Borges, others. Faithful English translations on facing pages. 352pp. 5⅜ × 8½.
25399-6 Pa. $7.95

THE CHICAGO WORLD'S FAIR OF 1893: A Photographic Record, Stanley Appelbaum (ed.). 128 rare photos show 200 buildings, Beaux-Arts architecture, Midway, original Ferris Wheel, Edison's kinetoscope, more. Architectural emphasis; full text. 116pp. 8¼ × 11.   23990-X Pa. $9.95

OLD QUEENS, N.Y., IN EARLY PHOTOGRAPHS, Vincent F. Seyfried and William Asadorian. Over 160 rare photographs of Maspeth, Jamaica, Jackson Heights, and other areas. Vintage views of DeWitt Clinton mansion, 1939 World's Fair and more. Captions. 192pp. 8⅞ × 11.   26358-4 Pa. $12.95

CAPTURED BY THE INDIANS: 15 Firsthand Accounts, 1750–1870, Frederick Drimmer. Astounding true historical accounts of grisly torture, bloody conflicts, relentless pursuits, miraculous escapes and more, by people who lived to tell the tale. 384pp. 5⅜ × 8½.   24901-8 Pa. $7.95

THE WORLD'S GREAT SPEECHES, Lewis Copeland and Lawrence W. Lamm (eds.). Vast collection of 278 speeches of Greeks to 1970. Powerful and effective models; unique look at history. 842pp. 5⅜ × 8½.   20468-5 Pa. $12.95

THE BOOK OF THE SWORD, Sir Richard F. Burton. Great Victorian scholar/adventurer's eloquent, erudite history of the "queen of weapons"—from prehistory to early Roman Empire. Evolution and development of early swords, variations (sabre, broadsword, cutlass, scimitar, etc.), much more. 336pp. 6⅛ × 9¼. 25434-8 Pa. $8.95

AUTOBIOGRAPHY: The Story of My Experiments with Truth, Mohandas K. Gandhi. Boyhood, legal studies, purification, the growth of the Satyagraha (nonviolent protest) movement. Critical, inspiring work of the man responsible for the freedom of India. 480pp. 5⅜ × 8½. (USO) 24593-4 Pa. $6.95

CELTIC MYTHS AND LEGENDS, T. W. Rolleston. Masterful retelling of Irish and Welsh stories and tales. Cuchulain, King Arthur, Deirdre, the Grail, many more. First paperback edition. 58 full-page illustrations. 512pp. 5⅜ × 8½.
26507-2 Pa. $9.95

THE PRINCIPLES OF PSYCHOLOGY, William James. Famous long course complete, unabridged. Stream of thought, time perception, memory, experimental methods; great work decades ahead of its time. 94 figures. 1,391pp. 5⅜ × 8½. 2-vol. set.
Vol. I: 20381-6 Pa. $12.95
Vol. II: 20382-4 Pa. $12.95

THE WORLD AS WILL AND REPRESENTATION, Arthur Schopenhauer. Definitive English translation of Schopenhauer's life work, correcting more than 1,000 errors, omissions in earlier translations. Translated by E. F. J. Payne. Total of 1,269pp. 5⅜ × 8½. 2-vol. set.
Vol. 1: 21761-2 Pa. $10.95
Vol. 2: 21762-0 Pa. $11.95

MAGIC AND MYSTERY IN TIBET, Madame Alexandra David-Neel. Experiences among lamas, magicians, sages, sorcerers, Bonpa wizards. A true psychic discovery. 32 illustrations. 321pp. 5⅜ × 8½. (USO) 22682-4 Pa. $7.95

THE EGYPTIAN BOOK OF THE DEAD, E. A. Wallis Budge. Complete reproduction of Ani's papyrus, finest ever found. Full hieroglyphic text, interlinear transliteration, word-for-word translation, smooth translation. 533pp. 6½ × 9¼.
21866-X Pa. $9.95

MATHEMATICS FOR THE NONMATHEMATICIAN, Morris Kline. Detailed, college-level treatment of mathematics in cultural and historical context, with numerous exercises. Recommended Reading Lists. Tables. Numerous figures. 641pp. 5⅜ × 8½.
24823-2 Pa. $11.95

THEORY OF WING SECTIONS: Including a Summary of Airfoil Data, Ira H. Abbott and A. E. von Doenhoff. Concise compilation of subsonic aerodynamic characteristics of NACA wing sections, plus description of theory. 350pp. of tables. 693pp. 5⅜ × 8½.
60586-8 Pa. $13.95

THE RIME OF THE ANCIENT MARINER, Gustave Doré, S. T. Coleridge. Doré's finest work; 34 plates capture moods, subtleties of poem. Flawless full-size reproductions printed on facing pages with authoritative text of poem. "Beautiful. Simply beautiful."—*Publisher's Weekly*. 77pp. 9¼ × 12. 22305-1 Pa. $5.95

NORTH AMERICAN INDIAN DESIGNS FOR ARTISTS AND CRAFTSPEOPLE, Eva Wilson. Over 360 authentic copyright-free designs adapted from Navajo blankets, Hopi pottery, Sioux buffalo hides, more. Geometrics, symbolic figures, plant and animal motifs, etc. 128pp. 8⅜ × 11. (EUK) 25341-4 Pa. $6.95

SCULPTURE: Principles and Practice, Louis Slobodkin. Step-by-step approach to clay, plaster, metals, stone; classical and modern. 253 drawings, photos. 255pp. 8⅛ × 11.
22960-2 Pa. $9.95

THE INFLUENCE OF SEA POWER UPON HISTORY, 1660–1783, A. T. Mahan. Influential classic of naval history and tactics still used as text in war colleges. First paperback edition. 4 maps. 24 battle plans. 640pp. 5⅜ × 8½.
25509-3 Pa. $12.95

THE STORY OF THE TITANIC AS TOLD BY ITS SURVIVORS, Jack Winocour (ed.). What it was really like. Panic, despair, shocking inefficiency, and a little heroism. More thrilling than any fictional account. 26 illustrations. 320pp. 5⅜ × 8½.
20610-6 Pa. $7.95

FAIRY AND FOLK TALES OF THE IRISH PEASANTRY, William Butler Yeats (ed.). Treasury of 64 tales from the twilight world of Celtic myth and legend: "The Soul Cages," "The Kildare Pooka," "King O'Toole and his Goose," many more. Introduction and Notes by W. B. Yeats. 352pp. 5⅜ × 8½.
26941-8 Pa. $7.95

BUDDHIST MAHAYANA TEXTS, E. B. Cowell and Others (eds.). Superb, accurate translations of basic documents in Mahayana Buddhism, highly important in history of religions. The Buddha-karita of Asvaghosha, Larger Sukhavativyuha, more. 448pp. 5⅜ × 8½.
25552-2 Pa. $9.95

ONE TWO THREE . . . INFINITY: Facts and Speculations of Science, George Gamow. Great physicist's fascinating, readable overview of contemporary science: number theory, relativity, fourth dimension, entropy, genes, atomic structure, much more. 128 illustrations. Index. 352pp. 5⅜ × 8½.
25664-2 Pa. $7.95

ENGINEERING IN HISTORY, Richard Shelton Kirby, et al. Broad, nontechnical survey of history's major technological advances: birth of Greek science, industrial revolution, electricity and applied science, 20th-century automation, much more. 181 illustrations. ". . . excellent . . ."—Isis. Bibliography. vii + 530pp. 5⅜ × 8¼.
26412-2 Pa. $13.95